THE
NEGATIVITY
FAST

ANTHONY IANNARINO

THE NEGATIVITY FAST

PROVEN TECHNIQUES
TO INCREASE POSITIVITY, REDUCE FEAR,
AND BOOST SUCCESS

WILEY

Published by John Wiley & Sons, Inc., Hoboken, New Jersey.
Published simultaneously in Canada.

For general information on our other products and services or for technical support, please contact our Customer Care Department within the United States at (800) 762-2974, outside the United States at (317) 572-3993 or fax (317) 572-4002.

Wiley also publishes its books in a variety of electronic formats. Some content that appears in print may not be available in electronic formats. For more information about Wiley products, visit our web site at www.wiley.com.

Library of Congress Cataloging-in-Publication Data is Available:

ISBN 9781119985884 (cloth)
ISBN 9781119985983 (ePub)
ISBN 9781119985907 (ePDF)

Cover design: Paul McCarthy

SKY10055182_091123

The acceleration of change in our time is, itself, an elemental force. The accelerative thrust has personal and psychological, as well as sociological consequences. . . . Unless man quickly learns to control the rate of change in his personal affairs as well as in society at large, we are doomed to a massive adaptational breakdown.

—Alvin Toffler, Future Shock

Our newfound knowledge leads to faster economic, social, and political changes; in an attempt to understand what is happening, we accelerate the accumulation of knowledge, which leads only to faster and greater upheavals. Consequently we are less and less able to make sense of the present or forecast the future.

—Yuval Noah Harari,
Homo Deus: A Brief History of Tomorrow

From a strictly mathematical perspective, the growth rates will still be finite, but so extreme that the changes they bring about will appear to rupture the fabric of human history.

—Ray Kurzweil, The Singularity Is Near:
When Humans Transcend Biology

Contents

Preface

As YOUR GUIDE for the Negativity Fast, my goal is to help you reduce the time you spend in a negative state and increase the time you are positive. At one time, I was terribly negative. To improve the quality of my life, I decided to remove the sources of negativity, including my own mindset. It helped me feel better and improved my outlook on life. I called this process the Negativity Fast. It worked, but I made a series of mistakes that I eventually corrected, including not fasting for long enough, not replying to negativity with positivity, and not recognizing that it is okay to be negative—but not all the time. Since then, I've developed a more structured approach to guide a 90-day Negativity Fast that anyone can adopt.

I've wanted to write this book for a long time. After the pandemic, I felt I had no choice but to write it for people who recognize that we are increasingly more negative than positive. It seems that the stress and anxiety of that tumultuous period are still present. Perhaps it has always been this way, and we needed that event to amplify how prevalent negativity is today. Our time on earth is short, and you don't want to waste it being negative. Negativity can harm your mental health, your physical health, and your relationships with others. In fact, sometimes we infect other people, including those we love, with our negativity, spreading it to them.

Our seven dominant emotions are anger, contempt, fear, disgust, happiness, sadness, and surprise. Five dominant emotions are negative, with happiness being the only positive one, unless the surprise happens to be positive. When you pay attention to the people around you at home, at work, or at your local Applebee's, you notice many folks are angry, contemptuous (especially around politics), fearful, or sad. You may also notice you are more negative than you used to be.

Before you start your Negativity Fast, you will need to learn strategies that will help you succeed with your fast. Without the chapters that come before the instructions at the end of this book, it will be more difficult to reduce your negativity and replace it with positivity. Each chapter provides practical, tactical strategies that will help you remove your negativity. There are several strategies in each chapter because some will fit you better than others. Different people will find different approaches work better for them.

It is also important that you know that I am not a medical professional, and nothing here is medical advice. Instead, you will find practical, actionable changes you can make to feel better. All the recommendations and strategies are supported by science. At the end of this book you will find a list of books and citations to scientific papers if you are so inclined to follow the science. I studied these strategies and adopted them so I could feel better and more positive, and now I want to share them with you.

We Are the People We Are Waiting For

WHEN YOU ARE getting ready to take off on an airplane, the flight attendant announces that should there be a change in cabin pressure, you should secure your own mask before helping others. You will not be helpful to others if you don't take care of yourself first. If there was ever a time to help each other, this is it. We need each other to make things better. The more of us who can reduce our negativity and replace it with positivity, the more we can help others feel better.

Here is an outline of what you'll read in this book:

- **Chapter 1: Why You Are Negative:** Without being overly scientific, we will start by looking at the science of why we are negative and how our current environment causes us to be more negative.
- **Chapter 2: Talking Yourself into a Negative State:** Here we will start to understand how we talk ourselves into a negative state and how to talk ourselves out of that state. Your inner voice isn't always helpful.
- **Chapter 3: Empathy and How to Lie to Yourself:** You will learn to lie to yourself in a way that can remove your negativity, especially when it comes to other people.
- **Chapter 4: How to Stop Complaining:** If you want to feel better more of the time, you will have to train yourself to stop complaining. Listen, if I can do it, you can do it.

- **Chapter 5: The Awesome Power of Gratitude:** This practice can help deal with depression. But don't take my word for it. Instead, we'll follow the example of the father of positive psychology.
- **Chapter 6: Reframing Negative Events:** You can loosen the hold that negativity has over you by reframing the negative events you have experienced. You did learn something that can turn a negative into a positive?
- **Chapter 7: How to Live Happily with Political Divisiveness:** Politics made me negative. It makes a lot of other people miserable. Here you will learn to be positive despite our extreme political divineness, no matter which party you support.
- **Chapter 8: Wanting and the Perils of Social Media:** After I wrote this chapter, I deleted the social media apps from my phone. You may want to share this with your children, especially teenagers.
- **Chapter 9: How to Change Your State:** There are a great number of things you can do change your negative state to a positive or neutral state. Your state is in your control.
- **Chapter 10: Minding Mindfulness:** This is short chapter about the benefits and strategies to practice mindfulness, something I learned from two Zen masters.
- **Chapter 11: How to Forget Your Problems and Concerns:** If you need to feel better fast, the easiest way to change that state is to help someone else, a strategy that will give you something called a helper's high.
- **Chapter 12: The Negativity Fast:** You'll identify your triggers and remove them as much as possible and replacing them with positivity.

You will find additional resources at www.negativityfast .com.

Disclaimer

I AM NOT a doctor or a medical professional. Nothing in this book is medical advice because I am not qualified to provide advice on medical issues. What you will find here are practical ways to reduce your negativity and spend more time being positive, making this a self-help book. I have practiced everything in this book myself and helped others with the advice and recommendations you will find in *The Negativity Fast*.

If you are depressed, overly anxious, or have thoughts about harming yourself or others, please reach out to a health-care provider for help. Here is a list of resources:

National Suicide Prevention Lifeline: 1-800-273-TALK (8255)
Crisis Text Line: Text HOME to 741741
SAMHSA's National Helpline: 1-800-662-HELP (4357)
Veterans Crisis Line: 1-800-273-TALK (8255)

Acknowledgments

I AM INDEBTED to Cher, my wife and best friend. She suffered years of me being angry and negative before I turned the corner and started to remove the sources of my negativity. No one supports me more than Cher.

I owe a debt and an apology to Aidan, my son, for teaching him to complain. I hope this book will undue the harm I caused. He is a better person than I was at his age or any age. He is a good man. Mia, my tall twin, and Ava, my small twin, are both positively positive girls, the result of their mother's influence far more than mine.

I am grateful to have a mom who never gave up on me. She is a wonderful mother, and even though I will never be able to match her contribution, I do my best to follow her example of charity and caring. Both my mom and my dad supported me from my teenage years playing rock 'n' roll in bars I was too young to be allowed in, to writing books like this one. I was never told that I couldn't do something, but when I was told not to do something, I was certain to do it.

I am also grateful to my sisters and brothers, Mike and Rachel and Mike, Thada and Rich and Josie, Molly and Jack and Max, Tara and Lindy and Abbigail, and my brother Jason and his outstanding contribution to Chapter 3: Empathy and How to Lie to Yourself.

My family at Solutions Staffing, Peg Mativi, Matt Woodland, and all the many people who help people who need work. Iannarino Fullen Group including Geoff Fullen and Brandy Thompson. My friend Beth Mastre. Jeb Blount, my partner in the OutBound Conference, where I previewed this book on the greatest sales stage of any sales conference. Victor Antonio for helping me be a better speaker and for allowing me to tease him, Mike Weinberg for his friendship, and Mark Hunter for always showing up. Andy Paul for being such a great host and thinker. Seth Godin for his friendship, influence, and his outstanding example.

When Shannon Vargo of Wiley acquired me as an author, I pitched her on the Negativity Fast. Shannon agreed to allow me to write something outside of sales, leadership, and business. This is my first book for a wide audience. I hope she forgives me for missing my due date, but some books are harder to birth, especially when one is overwhelmed with work. Christina Verigan straightens out my sentences and paragraphs and pushes me to make things clearer for the reader. She makes me a better writer. Deborah Schindlar, who produces my books with Wiley, is kind enough to chase me down and keep me on time. Thanks to Michael Friedberg for his help marketing *Elite Sales Strategies*, *Leading Growth*, and now, *The Negativity Fast*. John Acker has edited every book I have done with Wiley. John matches my irreverence and playfulness.

Most of all, I am grateful for you, the reader, who cares enough about the idea of going on a Negativity Fast and being more positive.

1

Why You Are Negative

IT'S NOT JUST you. Unless you've been sound asleep for the last quarter century, I'm sure you've noticed that most people are negative, grouchy, angry, and occasionally violent. Maybe you, like me, remember being more positive a few decades back. But it seems everyone around us is a lot more cynical and skeptical. Some people are even mad as hell. What happened?

Some of it is historical. The 21st century started with a terrorist attack on the United States, sparking a 20-year war in Afghanistan, which rolled right into the dot-com bubble, the Great Recession, sharper political divisiveness, a pandemic, supply-chain issues, a hot war in Europe, record inflation, and worst of all, reality television. And you wonder why everyone is a bit crabby.

To understand why we are negative and what to do about it, we must look to science to learn about the biology and psychology behind negativity. We'll also look through the eyes of a 20th-century futurist whose predictions about rapid social change are coming true. But if negativity wasn't helpful in some way, it wouldn't exist.

What Science Teaches Us About Negativity

I hesitate to talk about "the science" after the recent debates on masks, vaccines, lockdowns, and the like. But you need to know why you and I are wired for negativity. We'll start by exploring what psychologists label negativity bias. There are four components of negativity bias that you should know— but don't worry, I promise there won't be a quiz at the end of the chapter.

3

1. **Negative Potency:** Our negative emotions are stronger than our positive ones. If you've ever wondered why your negative emotional states seem to last longer than your positive ones, this may be part of the reason.
2. **Steeper Negative Gradients:** This intimidating term simply means that the closer a negative event, the faster your negativity about it grows. If you are anxious, it's likely you are focusing on some potentially negative future event. The odd thing is that this gradient is not nearly as steep for positive events.
3. **Negative Dominance:** Combining negative and positive events results in evaluations that are more negative than is logical or even justified. Guess what? You lost $100! Guess what else? You won $150. You sigh, more upset about the loss than happy about the $50 profit.
4. **Negative Differentiation:** In the real world, negative events are more varied and complex than positive events. Your brain uses more resources to think about, reflect, and process negative events. This leads to differences in the language we use to describe them and how we attend to, learn from, and remember them.

Because these elements work together, all humans have a negativity bias, even if some wallow in that negativity more than others. But psychologist Robert L. Leahy believes that evolution would not favor a trait that wouldn't help us survive: negativity is a feature, not a bug.[1] At the same time, we also have a bias towards optimism—a version of yin and yang. Yin and yang are chaos and order, light and dark, cold and hot, and up and down. Even though negativity is dominant, our optimism causes us to persist in pursuing our goals.

The Evolutionary Value of Negativity

Say you and I are cave people living tens of thousands of years ago. As we are walking around one day, you tell me you want to make a list of all the things that may cause serious problems. I like it: the reason you are my best friend is because you are always inventing new games like this one. "Okay," you say, "first question: Will this kill me?" I argue that the category is too broad since almost everything in our primitive environment is likely to kill us. Heck, half the things we eat would eat us if they had the chance.

Still, it's an important—and serious—question. How can we stay alive by avoiding things that might cause us to expire prematurely? So I propose a more specific test: "If I eat this, will I die?" You agree that food is difficult to come by, even if we aren't counting prehistoric carbs. I remind you that nine of our tribe members died after eating those enticing and delicious-looking red berries that grow near the waterline.

Since we know those berries are trouble, you suggest painting pictures of poisonous plants on the cave wall, as a warning to our friends and families. I remind you that five of our friends still ate the berries *after* the first group died. We agree that our tribe might think the drawings are a menu, so we decide not to publicize the berries any further. But we do need to be concerned about what we eat.

Next, you ask, "Will this person or persons try to dominate us?" Most of the cave dwellers close to us are real savages. Some of them don't bother to wear the fur from the animals they kill and eat, or even to follow Adam and Eve's cue and cover themselves with leaves. You and I are more civilized than these barbarians, and we also have a greater sense of fashion. We've been eating meat and our brains are expanding, even though the effects are not evenly distributed across the tribe.

As you are talking about the savages next door, I interrupt to suggest that whenever these neighboring brutes visit us, the first thing we should do is offer them those red berries. You object to taking their lives, as murder is wrong, perhaps even beneath us. I suggest keeping the berries around, just in case. Even if some of our neighbors are actually more friendly than violent, odds are that a bad egg will turn up eventually.

That point leads us to our next test: "Will this person copulate with me?" I think it's a crucial addition. As far as I can tell, this is our number-one priority, particularly since we enjoy spending more time with friends and less time with brutes. Our tribe tends to grow larger over time, but no one, even us, knows why half the tribe keeps finding crabby, loud, lazy, and squeaky people. It's a mystery, we decide, and chances are that no one will ever be able to explain it.

Before we head back to the cave, though, you make one final observation: Our optimistic peers don't seem to live very long. The ones who survived their impetuous actions have a lot of scars and broken bones. They often have trouble finding food, especially since they can't outrun anyone or anything. The few of us with gray hair tend to avoid rushing into things. We seem to be more pessimistic, skeptical, and cautious than the rest of our clan. Well, what's left of them anyway.

The ACDC Environment: Stress Under Constant Change

When I was a young kid playing rock 'n' roll, I was a dead ringer for Bon Scott, the legendary voice of AC/DC. Perhaps the future shock that Toffler predicted won't necessarily put us on the proverbial highway to hell, but it's worth thinking about another kind of ACDC: "Accelerating, Constant, Disruptive Change."

One reason that this change skyrockets our stress levels is that we weren't designed for this kind of environment. In the distant past, most of our immediate threats were high-grade stressors, like a saber-tooth tiger attack. Either you escaped or you became the tiger's dinner date. We didn't have the low-grade stressors of a boss, taxes, or car insurance payments for teenagers. Currently, however, most of our lives entail low-grade stressors, which we're ill-adapted to deal with.

At the time of this writing, for instance, our ACDC environment includes the following:

- The highest inflation numbers in more than 50 years
- High gas prices due to production and capacity issues
- Russia's war in Ukraine
- An increasing number of countries, led by China, choosing autocracy over democracy, making the world more dangerous
- An unchecked political divisiveness some suggest could lead to a US civil war
- The boomer generation retiring without enough workers to replace them, which is why you have bad service almost everywhere
- A low birth rate, just 54 births for every 1000 women in 2021
- Constant staffing challenges in health care (including nursing), despite having more than two jobs available (in the United States) for every person not presently working

- Speaking of work, technology's promise to help with work-life balance has instead exacerbated the problem, with people working day and night to keep up with their work
- Some in the sandwich generation who must take care of their children and their aging parents at the same time
- Increasing income disparity that may threaten our way of life.
- A decreasing life-span, largely due to suicide and drug overdoses

These major stressors often affect us directly, and they form the backdrop to our daily lives. While it may be possible to ignore at least of few of these, it's virtually impossible to forget them all completely. On top of these social and geopolitical issues, personal stressors add even more pressure. Even though these events may happen on a smaller scale, they loom larger in our lives because they are direct threats to what is most important to us. Here are a few examples:

- You are up for a promotion at work, and you're counting on the extra income, but your boss is considering promoting his current favorite ahead of you.
- Your seventh-grade daughter is being ostracized by the mean girls in her class, simply because she is a sweet, thoughtful, adorable, and bookish girl. She doesn't want you to intervene, but you can't stand to see her suffer.
- You feel an uncomfortable tickle at the back of your throat. Is it a cold? The flu? The latest pandemic? You can't afford to miss work now, but you can barely get out of bed.

- Three of your neighbors have reported break-ins this month. You wish you had the extra funds to upgrade your security system.
- Your 11-year-old wants a cell phone because all of his friends have one. You notice that his friends and your older kids are addicted to their phones. Even you have trouble putting your phone down. You want to do what is best but can't decide whether it's better to give him the phone so he can fit in or hold out until he's older and listen to him complain until then.
- The neighbor's kid with the long hair and the loud stereo drives too fast, and you're sure that one of these days he's going to hit one of the kids in the cul-de-sac. When you asked his parents to make him slow down, their "boys will be boys" defense didn't do your blood pressure any favors.
- Your car needs major repairs, but you can't afford a rental and the mechanic is fresh out of loaners.
- Your accountant called to say that the tax refund you were expecting was a miscalculation, and instead you owe money that you don't have.

Some of these smaller stressors stem from larger events, like inflation increasing a household's financial strain or political disagreements damaging personal relationships. Other stressors can simply be bad luck or part of a wider pattern of human behavior. Regardless of how stress enters our lives, we are all paying a price for the accelerating, constant, disruptive change. We feel the chronic stress and the toll it takes—not just in mental health outcomes like anxiety and depression, but in physical challenges like insomnia and heart disease. Couple that with ongoing psychological damage from technology and social media. We are bombarded daily with constant information, disinformation, and misinformation. A single "check out my vacation" picture can cause unhealthy social comparisons and ratchet up our fear of missing out.[2] It's even worse for young people, who often live on social media at a time when they are most developmentally vulnerable to comparison.[3,4]

Stress can cause problems with cognitive functions, like memory, attention, and decision-making. It can lead to a lack of productivity and efficiency in different aspects of our life. People with higher levels of neuroticism, including from genetic features, can be extra vulnerable to the negative effects of stress.[5,6]

One way to combat stress is to build resilience, so we can better cope with the challenges of living in an ACDC environment. Mindfulness can help, and so can building a strong social support system, to develop effective problem-solving skills. Later, we'll look at cognitive-behavioral therapy, along with tips for exercise, relaxation strategies, and finding work-life balance. It's also worth knowing that there are positive effects of stress, a concept called eustress (positive stress). Eustress can cause growth, greater creativity, and stronger performance, even in everyday people like you and me.

Negativity Is Biological

Your biology is sometimes the source of your negativity. Let's get real. You stay busy, often because you're taking care of everyone else. But failing to take care of yourself can multiply your stress and negativity. Our most basic animal needs are food, water, sleep, and movement. When we neglect those needs, we cannot effectively make decisions or use our higher-level cognitive skills. When our body is stressed, we aren't able to work on other important aspects of our lives.

Waiting too long to eat can send your body into a "hangry" state, inviting the three-pound, grayish-pink meatloaf that is your brain to unleash your inner Mr. or Ms. Hyde. Or perhaps you settled for an Oreo lunch because you were too busy to find a healthy meal. The sugar rush, you figured, was just what you needed to power through an afternoon of meetings. But just about the time John and Susan are rehashing the same argument they've had at every meeting for the past three months, your sugar high ends and you crash. For next time, I prescribe a small salad with some protein—and perhaps an urgent matter that requires you to miss the meeting. There are studies that suggest that a salad and protein for lunch can ward off negativity. They also suggest that a healthy food can cause a positive mood.[7]

My favorite way to ruin my biology (and mood) is to avoid drinking water. Your body is made up of around 30 trillion cells, and we carry around 36 trillion bacteria every day (gross, I know). All those cells and bacteria are thirsty. Recently, I stopped drinking coffee and sugar, replacing it mainly with water. It was terrible for two days, and then it was easy. You know those headaches you get in the afternoon? You might solve them by hydrating yourself and the colonies of bacteria depending on you. They're thirsty too![8]

Of all the biological sources of negativity, poor sleep is at the top of the stack, whether it comes from insomnia, the crying baby, or the two glasses of wine that shut down your liver for the night. Soon you'll wake up feeling not just groggy, but all set to be an extra on *The Walking Dead*—no makeup required. Getting more sleep can make you less irritable and more resilient, so you'll be better prepared to overcome negativity and stress.[9] Aim for at least seven hours per night, and more if you need it.

Avoiding exercise is another excellent way to turn off positivity while turning on negativity. You don't have to lift heavy weights like Arnold, or dive full-tilt into CrossFit in your late 40s (unless, of course, you enjoy rotator cuff surgery). Unless you are young, strong, and expect to be in a street fight, there is no reason to train for the UFC. Try walking or running for 30 minutes each day and lifting moderate weights. Science suggests that exercise can improve your attitude and cognitive functioning, not to mention the physical benefits.[10]

Negativity Is Psychological

Alvin Toffler may have been the first person to recognize the effects of rapid societal change in the modern era. In his popular book *Future Shock* (1970), Toffler wrote, "The acceleration of change in our time is, itself, an elemental force. The accelerative thrust has personal and psychological, as well as sociological consequences. . . . Unless man quickly learns to control the rate of change in his personal affairs as well as in society at large, we are doomed to a massive adaptational breakdown." Later, Toffler defined "future shock" as "the shattering stress and disorientation that we induce in individuals by subjecting them to too much change in too short of time." Sound familiar?

Like Toffler, I believe that the speed of change partly explains why we are more negative, pessimistic, cynical, skeptical, and perpetually outraged. Thanks to technology, globalization, and blurred lines between work and home, the nonstop world around us is partially responsible for the huge increase in mental health issues. We are more fearful about the future—anxious, worried, dislocated. And in the same way that fish do not know they live in water, we are unaware that our environment is constantly changing faster than we can adapt.

In *Future Shock*, Toffler predicted that we would have a tough time dealing with the rapid change he saw coming our way. He said we would have sociological and psychological challenges adapting to our environment. And he was right—just look around.

We look up to entrepreneurs who believe they should "move fast and break things," not recognizing who and what they are breaking, or even whether breaking it is a good idea. We are products of (and in) surveillance capitalism, where our data is the product. We're fed by our feeds, typically a steady diet of anger, body image problems, and even socially induced trauma like cyberbullying. Crisis after crisis plays out on the television news catwalk, and we mustn't miss Tuesday's fashion. And then there are the constant low-grade stressors that stack up on top of one another, until you can't even decide which one to worry about.

Fear is poison even in small amounts, and it can ruin your outlook on your life and your future. In a paper titled "Negativity Bias, Negativity Dominance, and Contagion," Paul Rozin and Edward B. Royzman note that "pollution always overtakes purity."[11] If a cockroach crawls onto your dinner plate, there's zero chance you'll dig in. When you read and watch poisonous media content every day, it's difficult to remove. It becomes a pattern of thought.[12]

In the last couple of years, our average life expectancy has dropped by several years, largely driven by fentanyl and suicide. Opioid abuse and suicide are both attempts to escape pain, mostly psychological pain. Along similar lines, home-lessness is reaching record numbers—drive through any large city, like Los Angeles, San Francisco, or even Austin, and you will be struck by how many people call the underpass home.

If you feel negative, part of the reason is the stress of liv-ing in this complex world that has been burning and turning for over four billion years. Despite Musk's desire to "travel to Mars," I am certain we are indigenous to this water-covered planet, moving through the universe at 600,000 mph while circling a giant ball of burning gas.

Before we go any further, I want to remind you that it is more than okay to feel and experience negative states. All our emotions exist because they are critical to our ability to live, survive, and thrive. Yes, we can be negative, but we can also show real compassion for others. So here's your first assignment: next time you feel negative, find someone who needs your help and see how fast your state changes to posi-tive. You picked up this book, so I have to believe that you want more out of life than a constant stream of stress.

Negativity Is Sociological

Another source of negativity is the people you encounter as you live your life—and yes, you're probably someone's source of negativity. When it comes to being difficult, for example, I am gifted in several areas. When someone tries to take advantage of me or bully someone weaker than they are, I can go from Mr. Rogers to Mr. T in two seconds flat. I try to avoid being a source of negativity, but sometimes I feel like a magnet for difficult people. It's like I have a sign on my forehead that says, "Come bring your drama to me!"

That's how I ended up fighting Steve Buckley—a 15-year-old neighbor kid who had at least 40 pounds on me—when I was barely 12. I'm still not sure what caused Steve to punch me in the first place, but I did learn that sometimes you end up in fights you didn't start. That was only one of many encounters with savages.

Sociological negativity may start at home, often with your siblings. I have two brothers and three sisters, and believe me when I say that my sisters were the toughest of any of us. Even after everyone is theoretically grown up, ostracism (or self-exile) can fuel familial negativity. Add in divorce, money problems, and the stress of work and raising children, and it's easy to understand why some families are a nest of negativity.

And then there's work. You knew we'd get here eventually, didn't you? Sure, you have some great coworkers. They're some of your best friends. But then there's Jimmy, that guy with a . . . difficult personality, let's say. He's always stirring the pot, sowing controversy, and creating conflict. He and a couple of his minions are clearly responsible for the negativity and the increasingly toxic culture in the office. No one knows why Jimmy gets away with his antics, but more than one coworker has noted a passing genetic resemblance between Jimmy and the boss.

Or maybe it's your boss who's the problem. As far as I can tell, bosses can be good or bad, but they're pretty much all grouchy. That's because they have significant responsibilities, including taking care of your paycheck. But you're still trying to read a hundred and forty emails a day (and that's not counting the texts, Slack messages, and casual questions from coworkers) and you send about four dozen emails yourself. Overwhelm is practically automatic. And it doesn't end at five. After you spend an hour or two in rush-hour traffic, you gulp down your dinner and spend at least part of your night "catching up," as if that were possible.

I've already given up watching the news on television. It's all negative, all the time, with practically nothing positive. If that changes, I might start watching again, but for now I'll stick to the funny cat videos my wife sends me on Instagram. Here's why: There really are compassionate and caring people in this world, but their stories rarely meet the standard of "If it bleeds, it leads."

If you live in the United States, you are one of the richest people on Earth. Most global citizens would happily trade places with you—especially if their daily experience includes subjugation, cruelty, famine, and war. Yet we perceive the negative because of negativity bias. Yes, our own society is a source of negativity, especially when it comes to the polarizing politics that divide us into two warring tribes. We'll come back to that later, but let's cool down a bit here for a minute. Today, many new human babies were born. Yay! People got married. Hooray! Someone landed a job they had dreamed of for years. Woot! And you, my friend, finally sat down to do something about your negativity.

Permission to Be Negative

Before we wrap up this chapter, I want to clarify one thing: You are allowed to be negative while you are working your way through this book—even during your negativity fast. You are a human being, and these states are natural. Feel free to experience, in whatever order you like, our common human emotions of anxiety, sadness, anger, frustration, guilt, shame, envy, jealousy, disappointment, and regret. For that matter, you might even stray into the negative states you like the best, like despair, inadequacy, embarrassment, alienation, hostility, hopelessness, or (some favorites) pessimism and cynicism.

You may have every reason to be anxious, which usually means you are worried about the future. If you are depressed, it often means you are focusing on the past; thank you, Lao Tzu, for that wisdom. Don't judge yourself by your negative states, especially when events around you might make negativity a perfectly appropriate response.

I am also claiming my right to experience negative states. I come from a family tree of practical stoics who had little if any interest in consoling anyone who felt sorry for themselves. My mother raised four children by herself. Her mother raised five children. Neither of these two strong women had any patience for sulking teenagers. I was never allowed to be depressed. It just wasn't on the menu. But I do have an easy time manifesting anger, irritation, hostility, and mistrust.

When I am in a particularly foul mood, I accept that I am in a negative state. Sometimes I just sit and enjoy noticing how unhappy I am. I normally do that away from my wife, Cher, because she doesn't tolerate my negative states. Eventually the state passes, and I can get back to being myself. It's okay to experience the moods and emotions, good or bad.

These states we all experience come and go like the seasons. You have good times where everything is going your way and you are mostly positive much of the time. Let's call them spring and summer. Other times, it gets dark early, the leaves fall off the trees, and things get cold and dry. Let's call them fall and winter. We've certainly had more fall and winter in the 21st century, but most of that is outside our control. Our job instead is to adopt a set of practical strategies so we can be more positive more of the time. Let's get to work on removing negativity.

2

Talking Yourself into
a Negative State

As a public speaker, I have to fly from Columbus, Ohio, to other cities for work. Many of my flights require connections in the airlines' hub cities. For example, flying on Delta means a trip to Detroit, Atlanta, or Minneapolis before boarding another flight to reach my destination.

I like flying because my iPhone is turned off for a couple of hours. I use the time in the cabin to write books, like the book you are reading now. I put on my noise-canceling headphones and type away while the miles fall away behind me. There is, however, a recurring travel experience that causes me to talk myself into a negative state: a flight delay, especially when I am headed home.

You may not have recognized that you routinely talk yourself into a negative state. Listen, I get it. You think your mental state changes because of other people and circumstances that you are not responsible for. But what if I am right, and you are incredibly adept at talking yourself into negative mood? I spent a chunk of my life being talked into being angry and upset by a voice that I alone can hear.

You know that voice that only you can hear? Yes, that one, the one that just said, "Yes, I know that voice." The voice in my head isn't very helpful when it comes to plane delays, whether they are due to weather or what the industry calls "a mechanical." (For mechanical issues, I am happy to wait for another plane.) No matter the reason, my voice works me into a negative emotional state. After all, it has had plenty of practice to perfect its talk tracks, taking me from zero to one hundred in mere seconds. It starts with catastrophizing the delay.

THE VOICE: You are going to be late getting home tonight.

ME: I know. I don't need you to remind me.

THE VOICE: You are supposed to land at 9:00 p.m., but now it's going to 11:30 p.m. You will not get the seven hours of sleep you need. On seven hours, you are the Dalai Lama. On five hours, you are Joseph Stalin. You should grow a bushy moustache.

THE VOICE: You are not going to have good energy tomorrow. You are never productive when you get home late. You'd feel better if you ate a bag of peanut butter M&Ms.

ME: I don't want peanut butter M&Ms! (Between you and me, I do really want those M&Ms, but I quit eating sugar.)

THE VOICE: No one has made an announcement. No one at the airline cares about you. Give them a piece of your mind. They don't respect you. Walk over and see if you see a plane.

ME: You know there isn't a plane there. You're just trying to wind me up. I'll call Cher to tell her I will be late.

THE VOICE: Fine. But that won't fix anything.

This voice isn't very helpful. It is incredibly negative—thank you, negativity bias. I must admire its dedication to its work, which is primarily to cause me to be negative. It's not the best person to travel with, especially while flying.

One trip home from the West Coast found me waiting for a flight at Chicago's O'Hare International Airport. I called Cher to tell her I would be home late, and I started complaining. Cher is a better person than I am, and after listening to me gripe about something I could do nothing about, she asked me, "If you had two free hours with nothing to do, what would you do with that time?" I told her I'd read a book, but I didn't have a book with me." She recommended that I walk to the bookstore and buy a book. Now I carry a large hardcover book on every trip, in case the Gods of Air Travel provide me time to read. You will find this theme repeated throughout this book: It is not a person or an event that causes you to be negative. Instead, it's your interpretation of these experiences. Your voice, if it is anything like mine, will work to make certain you perceive the event as negative.

Can you imagine what it must be like to work in customer service for an airline? The airline, of course, already knows it has a problem. They knew it before I did, and by the time I discovered the plane was delayed, they already sent a plane to pick me up as soon as possible. Maybe you don't fly enough to relate to my example. Here is one I am confident you know.

THE VOICE: Why does everyone drive so badly in [insert your city here]? It's like the first time they've ever had to drive in the rain.

YOU: C'mon! It's 65, not 45. What's wrong with you people?!

THE VOICE: That bastard cut you off. Honk the horn and give him a lesson in sign language.

YOU: People are crazy. He probably has road rage. No sign language!

THE VOICE: Looks like we will be sitting here for a while.

YOU: I know!

How to Examine Your Fears

Much of our negativity comes from our fears. My fear of getting home late is that I am not going to get the sleep I need to be productive. The truth of the matter is that nothing bad will happen because I am not as productive as I want to be. Other people have real fears, many worse than getting home late.

Imagine a single mom who is late to the daycare center, which fines her $10 for being late and an additional $1 for every minute she is late. If she doesn't have an additional $40 dollars for what is already one of her largest expenses, this fear is real. But even when she pays the fine, she is stressed, anxious, and she still must make dinner.

There are fears that come with real-world consequences and some that are simply an inconvenience. I am not a social scientist, but my experience is that our inner voice treats both events in the same way. We sometimes fear the wrong dangers, and in doing so our inner voice makes something more than it is. Much of the time when we are negative, it is because we are afraid. We are afraid of not getting the promotion, afraid of the neighbor's kid and his excessive speed, afraid of how our seventh grader is being treated by the mean girls in her class. Test this by noticing that when you are negative, much of the time it is because of something you fear.

Whose Voice Is It?

The voice that you hear in your head may not be your own. It is likely a composite of your parents, your teachers, your preacher, your boss, your significant other, and society.

These expectations your inner voice imposes on you can come from external sources. The idea that causes you to believe you must be productive every minute of the day isn't very helpful, especially when it comes to work-life balance. Many of the standards you observe weren't great for the people who practiced them and infected you with them in the first place. Many of their standards are their fears or something they picked up from other people.

All these sources that make up your composite inner voice may have imparted to you a set of rules you believe you must follow. Many of those expectations and rules serve you well, until they don't. No one—even the sources of your inner voice—has a perfect record of living by the expectations and rules they believe you should follow.

Because this is your one life on this earth, you must live it the best you can, and this means you need to examine your fears to determine when you are going to meet the voice's expectations and when you are going to ignore the voice altogether. Here is a famous example. The most-watched TED Talk on YouTube is Ken Robinson's "Do Schools Kill Creativity?"[1] Robinson tells the story of Gillian Lynne, the choreographer of *Cats* and *The Phantom of the Opera*. As a young girl, her mother took to see a specialist, because the school told her that Gillian had a learning disability. Gillian sat on her hands while the specialist spoke to her mother. The doctor turned on the radio and watched Gillian as she danced. The specialist told her mother that Gillian didn't have a learning disability. The specialist said Gillian was a dancer and to take her to a dance school, where Gillian thrived. She ended up a multimillionaire. Robinson said that today, we would put Gillian on an ADHD drug instead of sending her to dance school.

There are more stories about a parent who stopped their child from pursuing something they seemed to have little ability to do. In some cases, the parent may be cruel. But most of the time, the person's mother or father was trying to protect them from the harm of failure. Some of the pressure we feel comes from other people's expectations, their rules, and their fears. We must be cautious and not allow this inner voice to feed us other people's fears. We have enough as it is.

Ethan Kross is a psychologist and the author of a book titled *Chatter: The Voice in Our Head, Why It Matters, and How to Harness It*. Kross has spent his life studying "chatter." The research suggests that "when we experience distress, introspection often does significantly more harm than good."[2] The negative outcomes are many, including poor performance at work, making poor decisions, and harming our relationships with others.

Kross's research shows that "Chatter consists of the cynical negative thoughts and emotions that turn our singular capacity for introspection into a curse rather than a blessing." The voice is there for us when we need our inner coach. One strategy is to stop talking to yourself. If you are going to have a chattering inner voice, maybe trade your inner George Costanza for your inner Tony Robbins.

There are well-developed strategies that can help you lessen the negativity of your chatter, or what cognitive behavioral therapy (CBT) calls "your inner narrative." You narrate your situations, you create theories about people, and, naturally, you judge yourself. My inner narrative is always talking, often out loud.

CBT breaks your chatter into four categories that can be personified: the Worrier, the Critic, the Victim, and the Perfectionist.[3]

The Worrier

This chatterer says, "What if. . ." followed by the most horrendous outcomes. For some of us, just hearing something negative causes us to adopt a negative state, focusing on the worst-case scenario. Recently, one of my friends called and left me a voicemail telling me he needed to talk to me and that it was important. Immediately, my mind started to come up with different scenarios, each one worse than the one that preceded it. When we finally connected on the phone, I was already aware of what he shared with me, and it was nothing. My inner voice spent two hours coming up with terrible scenarios, none of which were close to the truth.

One strategy is to ask yourself if the situation is as bad as your imagination makes it. Think back on how many times you have worked yourself into a negative state only to discover that what you imagined was 10 times worse than what was true. This is how our negativity bias winds us up. One way to distance yourself from worry is to ask yourself if this will be important 10 years from now. Chances are, it won't be important an hour from now.

The Critic

If your inner voice tells you are not good enough, that is your self-critic. The critic will talk you down until you believe there is no reason to even try whatever it was you wanted to do. It may be a composite of all the voices that ever criticized you, or maybe a voice that isn't yours trying to protect you from being harmed.

I have published a blog post every day for 13 years at the time of this writing. Occasionally, someone criticizes my work.

When I first started writing, I would argue my point, trying to win my critics over. It didn't take long for me to realize that not everybody is going to love you, what you do, or how you do it. The good news is that you never have to worry about the opinion of people who are not going to attend your funeral. The negative opinions of others don't change who you are or what you are capable of. Have you ever noticed that the critic never creates? They are happy to criticize others at something they themselves have never done. The critic tells you more about them; some criticize you to feel better about themselves. Your inner critic creates only negativity.

The Victim

This narration is something like "I am hopeless." This is one way to put yourself in a negative state, while also disempowering yourself. This is the voice of the depressed. CBT would have you stop blaming others or making more of things than they are. I often wonder if we would be better off saving others than worrying about needing to be saved.

The Perfectionist

This narrative says, "I must do everything perfectly, even if I am not happy (Enneagram 1, the angriest of the three anger types). Not only is this state exhausting to the perfectionist, but it's also exhausting to everyone around them. The perfectionist believes everyone must be perfect or their mistakes will come back on them.

Strategies from Cognitive Behavioral Therapy

CBT is a set of helpful strategies to remove or lessen your negative state. The first strategy I have practiced is identifying whether the thought is specific or general. If you want to be negative, take something specific and make it general. Like this:

General: I hate my job!

Maybe you hate your job. Or maybe you are making yourself miserable because you are generalizing, and by doing so, making things worse. All generalizations are lies (even this one). To reduce the chatter, get specific.

Specific: Lately, I have had too much administrative work.

I am allergic to administrative work. A single form from a government entity can cause heart palpitations, hives, difficulty breathing, until I finally pass out. It's worse at tax time. Let's just say, I prefer not to fill out any forms.

The second strategy I have practiced is to identify if something is temporary or permanent. I have watched salespeople take a temporary setback and make it a permanent condition.

Permanent: "I suck at sales. I need to do something else." But what if you don't suck at sales and this is an ordinary, run-of-the-mill sales slump. Instead, you could frame this experience as temporary.

Temporary: "I am in a sales slump. I need to double my effort and work through this." It would be a rare occurrence that one might lose their competency overnight.

Ethan Kross would tell you, "When we are upset, we tend to over-focus on receiving empathy rather than find practical solutions." If you can do something to improve your situation, do it. If you can't do anything about it, let it go.[4]

Talking Yourself Out of a Negative State

If you can talk yourself into a negative state, doesn't it make sense you should be able to talk yourself out of a negative state? If you can accomplish a negative state by listening to a voice that is wildly too pessimistic, what would stop you from listening to the optimistic voice that believes in you without a hint of doubt?

The Voice's Track Record

If you want to work on your inner narrative, you might write down the negative outcomes it suggests are all but certain. Keep this list and write down the very few negative events that come true, even though I bet you'll have difficulty remembering when your "chatter" got a call right. If your inner voice is ever correct, immediately buy as many Mega Millions tickets as you can afford, as the odds are about the same.

Recall the last time your "chatter" showed up to tell you that the only outcome available is a terrible, negative outcome that will surely harm you. But you are here now, reading this book while your inner voice scoffs at these strategies, believing it has the upper hand in this contest. It's worth remembering that your inner narrative is one of the world's worst futurists.

If you pay attention to your inner narrative's propensity to catastrophize the tiniest worry or concern as it was the worst possible thing ever to happen to you, you'll notice how outrageous your inner dialogue is. You inner voice is hyperbolic, exaggerating its claims without any real evidence or proof of its prediction. Your inner narrative is way, way, way overconfident, which is how it cows you into being anxious about something that hasn't happened, and most likely won't happen at all.

The last thing you should do if have you have a hyperactive and excitable inner voice is watch television news. Watching the news feeds the monster with stories it can use as fuel to cause you to feel afraid. The story about this nice person who had this terrible event is certain to be your fate, says your inner voice, even if the odds are so low they can't be measured.

You are still here, even though your inner narrative can't understand how this is possible. After all the bad things that could or should have happened over all these years, you are still here, still going strong, but maybe just a bit more negative than you want to be.

Positive Affirmations

Look, if you are going to vanquish your negative inner narrative, you need to be reminded of how good you really are. This is a contest you are going to win, but just in case, I am going to ask you to do a little work to be more than certain. You have more successes than failures. But a negativity bias causes us to remember our negative events better than we remember our positive outcomes. The positive events and experiences are not well documented. Let's start by making a list of your accomplishments.

Recall a time you were worried about a big, important job interview for your dream job. Then you nailed the interview and were hired for your dream job. This is the eustress, the positive stress we experience (Chapter 1). Not all stress is bad.

At some point, you asked a special person to join you for a dinner date. The date turned out to be the love of your life. You have been together since that day.

Maybe you tried out for theatre in college and was cast as the main character, even though you weren't ready to be the lead. The reviews were outstanding, even though you didn't turn out to be the next Al Pacino.

In Anne Lamont's outstanding book on writing, *Bird by Bird*, she recommends writers make a list of all their stories. In some way, we are our stories. Because we are at the beginning of this book, you should write down only the positive stories and events of your life. Start with the idea of being born, a miracle of miracles. As you recount all the good in your life, without you noticing, this walk down memory lane will remind you of the negative experiences and events. Nod in their direction and go back to building a counternarrative you can use to remind the voice that you alone can hear that you have been blessed to have had many positive experiences.

Later, after we build up our immunity a bit more, you can write down the negative stories when they have less power over you. Some of my best stories are negative events, each of them causing me to grow from the stress and the exposure, a few of them violent. Because you have survived every negative event up until now, they can no longer harm you.

In the meantime, you can use affirmations to argue with your negative voice. When it tells you that you are not good enough for whatever it is you want to do, simply respond, "Even though I have no idea how to do this, I am smart enough to figure it out." The voice tells you that you are going to be hurt; explain that you have been hurt before, and if something bad happens, you'll work through it. Some part of your negative inner dialogue is trying to protect you. Without any proof, I believe that voice comes from an older part of the brain, maybe your subconscious, as it is responsible for a large part of everything you do. It works to keep you alive, and it is hypervigilant when it comes to threats. Thank it for doing its work keeping you safe.

There is evidence that positive affirmations can reduce your negativity and stress. It turns out that writing about your core values can weaken the implications of a threat.[5] If you remember negative differentiation, the phenomenon that your negativity grows the closer the danger, this can help. Self-affirmations can be useful for reducing negativity and stress, but the effectiveness may depend on individual differences. Here is a list of powerful affirmations, according to Google:

I am successful.
I am confident.
I am powerful.
I am strong.
I am getting better and better every day.
All I need is within me right now.
I wake up motivated.
I'm rising above the thoughts that are trying to make me angry or afraid.
My personal favorite: I am blessed to be loved and to share my love.

The Science of Inner Dialogue

There is plenty of good science in this chapter, thanks to Ethan Kross. But I found one paper that provided a way to understand self-talk and inner dialogue. The difference can help you use each one in a helpful way.

A 2020 study by Piotr K. Olés and colleagues[6] looked at relationships of self-talk and internal dialogue. Self-talk and inner dialogue are two ends of a continuum. The easiest way to understand the difference between self-talk and inner dialogue is that in self-talk you are playing both the sender and the receiver. When you are engaged in inner dialogue, you include other voices: your friends, a family member, lost relatives, teacher, mentors, media stars, or some other voices.

- **Self-Talk:** Self-talk is generally brief and task or goal focused. In this case, the self-talk is self-reinforcement. This is a single "I-position." It might sound like, "I can do this, but I am going to need more time."
- **Internal Dialogue:** Internal dialogue is complex and has several "I-positions." This tends to be a confrontational and often self-critical. It could sound like, "I should get started on this project. I should get some exercise first. Last time you waited too long, you were stressed out. What about work-life balance?"

There are a number or types of inner dialogues, including identity dialogues like values, and life choices. We also engage in social dialogues. These dialogues are part of future or past conversations. This helps us prepare for conversations, discussions, and create alternative scenarios.

The research shows that we benefit from internal dialogue, and they help us achieve goals, like motivating ourselves.[7] If we are trying not to make the mistake again in the future, we may benefit from confrontational inner dialogue.

Do This Now

- Notice when you are engaged in self-talk and when you are having an inner dialogue. Try to be positive when engaged in both different ways we talk to ourselves.
- Write a list of your accomplishments to remind you and the negative voice you carry around in your head that things aren't nearly as negative as your voice pretends it to be. If you are the type of person who doesn't give yourself credit, you may have to practice, even though you have plenty of successes.
- If you have a problem, get to work trying to solve it because that will help you stay positive. (This is one of the strategies from *Chatter* by Ethan Kross.) You are better off dealing with it.

3

Empathy and How to Lie
to Yourself

AT THE BEGINNING of each new year, the gym next to my go-to Starbucks is packed. The first week of January finds the parking lot stuffed with people, all decked out in new gym clothes and hauling oversized water bottles, showing up early to keep their commitment. Every week after that, the crowds thin out a little more. Halfway through February, you could park right in front of the door.

Maybe you weren't in that "I'm going to hit the gym every morning" crowd. Perhaps, instead, you vowed to give up soda or only eat salad or finally learn Portuguese. Whatever your resolution was, chances are you lied to yourself about it. Sometimes our intentions are good, but as humans we can't help being fallible.

If you are going to lie to yourself, you may as well tell the kind of lie that improves your life by making you less negative. Maybe you don't yet believe that lying to yourself can remove the negativity that stems from other people's actions, but hear me out on this.

You see, sometimes we're negative precisely because we lie (even just to ourselves) about other people. We insist that they're intentionally creating problems for us, and that malice can be their only motive. You know the patterns. That woman who insists on chatting with the grocery cashier is deliberately holding up the line. That guy driving 20 miles per hour below the speed limit is deliberately endangering everyone around him. And of course, your neighbor is deliberately leaving his dog outside all day, even though he knows it'll bark at every passing car and squirrel.

Maybe It Isn't Road Rage

My younger brother, Jake, is a professional comedian. More specifically he is a dirty comedian and insult comic. You may have seen Jake in *The Animal* and *The Hot Chick*, both movies starring Rob Schneider. Jake started in comedy when he was 17. It is all he has ever done. At one point he had a girlfriend who urged him to get a legitimate job or she would leave him. He worked in a call center for a couple hours, but ultimately chose comedy over the girlfriend. (I say Jake is a dirty comic, so if you decide to see him, you can't say I didn't warn you. If you sit in the front row, I will pray for you. You will need the prayers.)

Like me, Jake must travel to his gigs, often driving long distances to get there and driving back home after his show. Jake always struggled with other drivers, often telling me that Florida really does have the worst drivers in the entire world. (It's true!)

Often, Jake finds himself miles away from the next rest stop, keeping his fingers (and legs) crossed that he can make it before his bladder overloads. In those moments, he's not thinking about courteous, defensive driving—he's just got to go. One day, Jake noticed a car behind him weaving in and out of traffic, eventually winding up beside Jake's car. At first, Jake got upset. Who did this idiot think he was?! But then he got a look at the driver's pained expression, and it was all too familiar. His fellow motorist was afraid he wasn't going to make it to the next rest stop.

Instead of staying angry, Jake honked the horn and waved the driver to get in front of him. He even rolled down the window and yelled, "Go, you can make it!" If Jake hadn't had more than a couple close calls of his own between Columbus, Ohio, and some small town in Iowa, he might not have been so empathetic. From that day forward, Jake decided to lie to himself and believe anyone driving poorly was experiencing the same problem he had on the road, rather than believing they were horrible, dangerous drivers. So, if you see a guy in a red Cadillac waving you into traffic, wave and say hello to Jake or ask him to escort you to the rest area.

Here's my point: One way to reduce your stress is to lie to yourself about *why* people do things that bother you. Heck, the motive you imagine might even be true. Maybe that grocery-line slowpoke recently lost her husband and doesn't have anyone at home to talk to. Maybe that slow driver just got his license and is not quite used to the interstate yet. You can even make it into a game—who can come up with the best explanation for bad behavior? My go-to guesses are low blood sugar or a notice from the IRS announcing an audit. Or maybe the people around you are just having a tough day. If you can remember a time when you were not at your best, even in public, you can empathize with them rather than throwing the first stone. And empathy makes it hard to stay mad at strangers for long. (Family may be a bit more difficult.)

Empathy Without Knowing Why

In business today, everybody talks about how people should have more empathy. But you don't always have to know why people act the way they do, especially when their actions are unproductive, unhelpful, or even harmful. While I believe that empathy is a nice idea, it isn't the high-water mark of caring. But empathy is a skill, and like most skills we can break it into several components.

Emotional Sharing

This means you feel the same emotions as the other person. You may have had this experience with a friend or a family member, or even when watching a TV show or movie.[1] Once, for example, I was moved emotionally during a play. A character experienced something that was so close to one of my negative childhood events that I felt the exact same emotions I had felt when I was seven years old. You can use this type of empathy to put yourself in another person's situation. Take their perspective, not your perspective—and recognize that your negative perspective may not be helpful for either of you. It may, in fact, be worse because you are now full negative.

Perspective Taking

This empathy is different. It is a cognitive empathy, one that has you thinking and understanding another person's perspective. This is often what we mean when we talk about empathy in business: understanding another person's thoughts and feelings without the active emotional sharing.

Empathic Concern

This kind of empathy prompts us to help when people are suffering, like when you see someone struggling and you decide to help them pick up the oranges that fell out of their grocery bag. Empathic concern may or may not prompt emotional sharing, but it does cause us to act to help others.[2]

Emotional Regulation

This is your ability to manage your own emotions while dealing with someone who is emotional. Some people, maybe you, are so empathic that they can find empathy distressful and overwhelming.[3] I have a sister who falls apart when others are struggling. This is because she has trouble separating her own emotions from the emotions she's seeing in others.

Responsiveness

This one's simple: you communicate that you understand, validate, and care for the person you are empathizing with.

Now that you know more about empathy, you can use it to respond less negatively to behavior that bothers you. You don't need to know exactly what prompted that person to act that way, but you can imagine an activating event that requires you to be empathetic. Recognize that a person in a better state would not have done whatever they did that you allowed to trigger you.

Finally, remember that in some cases, empathy will not work—you need compassion. If empathy requires walking a mile in the other person's shoes, compassion recognizes that those shoes are two sizes too small and helps them get shoes that fit. Compassion is more than just understanding the person's feelings and thoughts; it's trying to help alleviate their pain.

Albert Ellis's ABC

Albert Ellis was an expert on anger management and the originator of both Cognitive Behavioral Therapy and Rational

Emotive Behavior Therapy (REBT). His several books include *How to Keep People from Pushing Your Buttons* and *How to Control Your Anger Before It Controls You.*

You may believe that others are pushing your buttons, but you are pushing these buttons yourself. What Ellis was able to see was the patterns people practiced. Ellis used the letter pattern ABC to describe how you wind yourself up:

- **A is for the activating event:** Specific situations or people that trigger the process.
- **B is for your beliefs and feelings about the activating event:** These are what winds you up, not the activating event. It's true!
- **C is for consequences:** These are the feelings and behaviors that arise based on how you respond to the event.

You have already seen this pattern in the story of my brother Jake deciding that the bad driver was driving poorly because he was in a bit of a hurry. All Jake did was change his belief about the driver to remove the emotions and his negative feelings.

We often act as if A, the activating event, causes our feelings and behaviors. Ellis would tell you that As don't create Cs, even though up until this page, you may have had no awareness that you create the C by your beliefs and feelings about the activating event.

Ellis focused on the B, the beliefs. He wrote, "What do we do at point B when we run into a difficult situation or person at point A before we wind up feeling or acting in Point C?" He continued, "There are lots of words to describe what we do at Point B: we react, choose, perceive, decide, analyze, make a judgment, size up the situation, assess it, imagine—all these words fall under one rubric, one umbrella term: WE THINK!"[4]

Here is a common activating event: I receive a form from a government office that requires me to fill in a few boxes. My belief is that "these people are stealing my time." How's that for an unproductive belief about paperwork? My C is that I become angry at being asked to complete a form. I could choose a less harmful behavior, like frustration instead of anger. What I do now is save all administrative work and bills and complete them on Financial Friday, my way of dealing with bureaucrats and government paper pushers (who still steal my time).

Speaking of frustration, people who have shared a house with teenagers have gone from A to C, skipping past B, when one of these little monsters provides you with an activating event. You may respond by being angry, without thinking at all. But if you pause and think, the bad behavior may be something that should cause you to be concerned. If you can remember back to when you were a teenager, you can be empathetic remembering how stressful it was to fit in. That may be a better response, one that may help you teenager talk through what really has them upset. It doesn't mean that you can't take their car keys or send them to a military academy or a nunnery somewhere on the East Coast. Those are always options after you go back and work your way through B. Even if you decide against them, they can at least be useful threats.

Mind your Bs. Your beliefs are what wind you up. When people tell you should not lie, remember that we all lie to ourselves. Sometimes, your beliefs are dead wrong.

Seeing What Is Invisible

When I was a young businessman, I won a big client. I had just opened a new location of my family's staffing business, and I needed this account to anchor the new office. My contact was an incredibly difficult person. Even though we were doing a good job, she was always unhappy about something. She would curse at me, threaten me, and rip me to pieces daily. I was thick-skinned, and I never retreated. I showed up every day to take care of the client.

One day, my highly emotional client fell into her chair and confessed: "Between working 12-hour days here and sleeping in a chair next to my husband who has already had two surgeries for his cancer, I don't know how much more I can take." In that moment, I understood she was suffering and afraid.

As she disclosed her family's battles, I told her not to worry about the business, and that I would make sure she had the employees she needed to run the business. Our relationship changed that day, and I learned that there are invisible forces all around us. While you and I may not be able to teach this to all eight billion of us, at some time or an another, we are all fighting battles that are invisible to others.

Another time, a great friend of mine called me on a Sunday morning. He asked me how I was, and I told him I was awful, as my sump pump failed, and my basement was flooded. As I finished telling him about the basement, he told me that one of his best friends and her family died in a plane crash. One daughter wasn't with her parents and her sister, and she lost her entire family. I stayed on the phone with my friend for hours, knowing that talking to him was more important than the carpet that was destroyed in the flood. I could imagine how he felt, and it was enough for me to forget about what had been my own problem. My belief had changed in a moment.

In both scenarios, what was there in front of me was invisible to my eyes. There was an activating event (A) I couldn't see and my belief (B) was not accurate with the limited information I had. Once confronted with the activating event, the consequences I recognized (C) changed in a second.

I spend a great deal of my time trying to see what is invisible to others. I am certain you have had these experiences too.

Don Miguel Ruiz wrote a wonderful, powerful little book called *The Four Agreements: A Practical Guide to Personal Freedom (A Toltec Wisdom Book)*. I recommend the audiobook, which is read by the actor and Zen master Peter Coyote. He has the perfect voice for the book. Ruiz's Third Agreement is "Never Make Assumptions." I believe this agreement needs a slight change to: "Don't assume bad intentions, and instead practice empathy and give the person the benefit of the doubt. They may be doing the best they can."[5] If you are going to attribute intentions to a person, make them good intentions and hope that others do the same for you when you are struggling and not at your best

You may have noticed life isn't easy. You are shot out of the womb and must learn all kinds of things to be a decent human being. It's easy to get a lot of things wrong. Without meaning to, you harm others; sometimes others harm you. Those of us who need grace from time to time should extend that grace to others. If you are going to make assumptions about people, the best one you can make is that they would do better if they could, but something in their past brought them to where they are now. Prosocial behavior supports positive relationships, strong social ties, and enjoyable interactions with others. The key to prosocial behavior is giving other people the benefit of the doubt, and treating people with kindness without expecting a reward.[6]

There is nothing you can do about other people. They will do what people do. Some are kind, helpful, and polite. Others are angry, difficult, and negative—and even more so post-pandemic. The only person you have some control over is you. The stimulus doesn't control you, so don't react to it automatically. In *The Seven Habits of Highly Effective People*, Stephen Covey reminds us that there is a space between the stimulus and your response. This is the space of beliefs in Ellis's ABC. One way to lessen your negativity is to use that pause to determine what the stimulus really means. The more meaning you invest in it, the more certainly you will trigger your own negative state. For example, if you believe a person is giving you a hard time because they disrespect you, your response will be driven by negative feelings. By contrast, if you believe the person's attitude is due to some misfortune in their personal life, you can respond with compassion.

Radical Acceptance

It would be a mistake to leave out certain important strategies that can help you with deal with other people. One of these strategies is called radical acceptance. It reminds me of mindfulness in some ways, because it requires you to let go of the illusion of control and accept things as they are without judging. This concept originates with Buddhism and was introduced to Westerners by Marsha Linehan, the creator of dialectical behavior therapy (DBT).[7] It was designed to help people with borderline personality disorder. You can use this by acknowledging your feelings and your emotions without judging them. You can also name your thoughts and what you are telling yourself. Then challenge your belief about what these things mean and let them go.

You might have a difficult person or an event that triggers negativity. By accepting that it is what it is without judging it, you let it go. You don't have to agree with a person or forget or forgive. Radical acceptance allows you to set it down and leave it right where it is. Being able to accept things as they are, you accept that someone or something isn't fair or that something should be different.

I have never personally cared much for reality. Like you, my world isn't exactly how I'd want it to be. I wasn't given so much as a chance to make suggestions about how the universe should work. As far as I have been able to discern, reality isn't worried whether you and I approve of how things work on Planet Earth. You can pretend to play God and list out all the things you believe should be different, but it will only make you more negative. Here is a list of things you should leave behind:

- **Beliefs that no longer serve you:** One of the ways that we grow is by changing our beliefs. The longer we hold on to our outdated beliefs, the longer it takes to adopt new beliefs. One way to keep track of your growth as a human adult is to make note of the beliefs you have left behind. When you hear people suggest that someone flip-flopped, you should recognize they saw something with new eyes. You can do the same.

- **Your willingness to rationalize:** Stop attributing negativity to external factors. When you were a child, you didn't want to get in trouble. You would blame others for whatever mischief you were caught up in. It's better to attribute your negativity to yourself, not others. If Ellis teaches us anything, it is that we make ourselves angry and negative. At some age, this gets easier because you care less.
- **Procrastination:** Act when it is necessary and when you can make a difference. This chapter is about empathy and lying to ourselves. In a later chapter, we'll take a deep dive into how making a difference can cure you of your negativity.
- **Small choices:** Treat negativity as a small choice and make choices that empower you to be positive. The big choice is one that allows you to be positive when you feel negativity. If I am negative, it shows on Cher's face. That's how I know that I have made a small choice when a bigger choice would be better. If you are a man, you know this look. And ladies, you know when that look is necessary—or perhaps your significant other gives you that look.
- **Your fears:** You fears can cause negativity. The more you can leave your fears behind, the easier it will be to be positive.
- **Negative people:** You may have to leave negative people behind, at least until you complete your Negativity Fast.

Assertive Communication

I am very comfortable with conflict. I've done the work to be able to control my response to triggers, but occasionally I can be defensive when challenged. This is one of the problems of being an Enneagram 8, so I try to be a 9, a peacemaker.

This is a more direct way to deal with certain difficult people in a way with less conflict and more collaboration.

Without being negative and without trying to create more conflict, you have the right to express your needs and set boundaries. By effectively communicating your boundaries, you can reduce your negativity while also defending yourself from people who take advantage of you, take you for granted, or treat you poorly. First, be clear and candid about your boundaries. Because people can't see your boundaries, you must remind them where they are. Learn to say no, politely but with resolve. I am incredibly sensitive to people taking advantage of me, and I have to try to be polite and professional, though I often fail.

Whenever you must have a difficult conversation, write out everything you want to say in bullet points. Then test it on people you believe will tell you where you have gone too far, and where you might make a change. Then practice it and get comfortable with the words coming out of your mouth.

You can be completely professional while also defending yourself by saying something like, "I am going to ask you not to speak to me that way," or "I will not allow you to treat me this way." When you need to set a boundary, it's best to be calm and clinical, showing no emotion at all. (It's scary when you say something with absolutely no emotion.)

Avoidance

When I was young, I hung around with the wrong kind of people. I found trouble, and when I didn't, trouble found me. Until one night, I had a premonition that I would die before I turned 25. Once I decided to change my life and my future, I chose to avoid people who would bring me trouble.

You can—and should—avoid people who are negative, as they can make you negative. Difficult people are also worth avoiding; they can create more negativity. Here are some people you might want to avoid: gossips, the untrustworthy, people who lack integrity, users, critics, backstabbers, people who spread rumors, bullies, victims, and people who dress up as clowns (it's scary).

How to Let Go

An average life in the United States is about 4,108 weeks in total. You might be incredulous about this statistic. On average, we live 77.28 years. That's 4,108 weeks in total. Life expectancy moved up a few years when people stopped smoking. Recently, it's moving down for three reasons: suicide, fentanyl, and COVID-19. In 2021, over 70,000 people died from fentanyl alone. Alcohol, drugs, and suicide claimed 186,763 Americans in 2022.[8]

You and I are likely to have more than 4,018 weeks because we live in the United States and wouldn't go near anything like fentanyl. So what are you going to with your allotted time on Planet Earth?

I have an app called Countdowns, which I bought to track my deadlines, but not for this book, which is way late. One day, I decided that I would shoot to live to at least 82 years, which means at the time of this writing, I have 1,377 weeks remaining, but I will press for more, as I very much like it here.

When I tell people the number of weeks I have remaining, some think it is morbid. Listen, your birth is a death sentence. In the words of the great Jim Morrison, "No one here gets out alive." For me and the Zen Buddhists, this is a form of liberation. I hope you recognize that because you have only so much time here, you should let go of the sources of negativity.

All the people I love are here. All the people who love me are here. I still have work to do. My office and my basement hold all the books I still need to read. Sadly, you can't read nearly as many books as you might want. At one a week, I can read 1,377 books.

While you are here, there is no reason not to enjoy your time, eat good food, spend time with people you love, travel, and do all the things you want to do. Forgive the people who harm you and apologize when you harm others. Wait! You didn't realize that, occasionally, you are the person who creates the activating event? C'mon, you know that sometimes you can be a difficult human being, don't you? I am attributing good intentions to your negative events.

The Science of Empathy

In a 2021 paper titled "Empathy: A Clue for Prosociality and Reciprocity," by von Bieberstein and colleagues,[9] the authors propose empathy is a clue for prosociality, and people are generous to people they believe empathetic. To test this theory, the authors conducted a study where the participants were required to complete a series of tasks. One task had them completing the Interpersonal Reactivity Index (IRI). This test calculated their empathy.

Another task was a dictator game where the person could give another person a sum of money or keep it all for themselves. Those who scored high in the IRI were more likely to share money in this game.

What is more is that the participants shared money with people they believed were empathetic. When the participants were high in empathy, they overestimated how much they shared with others. "These findings suggest that empathy can influence how we perceive others' prosocial behavior, and that this can in turn influence our own prosocial behaviors."[10]

Empathy can promote indirect reciprocity. This is a social interaction where people are rewarded for being helpful to others, even when the help isn't directly reciprocated. "These findings suggest that empathy can influence how we perceive others' prosocial behavior, and that this can in turn influence our own prosocial behaviors."[11]

Empathy can help us take the perspective of another, making us more tolerant and encouraging us to feel compassion for others. This supports prosocial behavior, like helping one another, even when there isn't any tangible benefit to us. Empathy can also help us feel connected to others, reducing feelings of isolation and loneliness. Empathy can make us less negative and more positive overall.

Another paper, by Wang and colleagues, looks at 200 male offenders in China.[12] The ones who had more parental care and encouragement had higher levels of "cognitive and affective empathy." Offenders who had inconsistent parenting styles had lower levels of empathy.

I grew up surrounded by male offenders without a father at home. One day I was walking home with another kid from my neighborhood. We were a long way from home, and he spotted two bicycles lying in the front yard of a house. My neighbor said we should take the bikes. I kept walking, but he went back and stole a bike. When I asked what he did with the bike, he told me he threw it in the dumpster. Last I heard, he was in prison in San Quentin.

How to Exercise Your Empathy In Advance

- Lie to yourself about a person's motives when they are the activating event unless they aim to harm you or others. In that case, your empathy needs to extend to others.
- Know that everyone you meet is fighting a battle you can't see. If you knew their backstory, you'd be more empathetic. Go ahead and write their backstory yourself. If Jake can do it, and if I can do it, you can do it too.
- Take no offense. I will likely repeat this until you share it with everyone you know or tattoo it on your forearm: *You never have to worry about people who are not going to be at your funeral.* Let things go that don't truly harm you.
- It takes time and practice to let go of the sources of negativity. The primary purpose of this book is to help you let things go. You don't have to invest your time and your emotional energy in things that aren't worth the time.

4

How to Stop Complaining

THERE IS NOTHING better than a newborn baby. We had three of them, first one, and then two. All three were born while I was working full time and going to law school. I asked our doctor if twins was from one side of the family. Apparently, I didn't learn much in my biology class in high school. She explained there are always a billion swimmers. My wife dropped multiple eggs; the doctor warned us we could have twins or triplets. This was the conversation that ended any ideas about having more babies.

As cute and lovable as babies are, you might have noticed they are awfully grouchy. They spend a lot of their time in negative states, spreading that state to their sleep-deprived parents. Babies complain for one overarching reason: They can't do anything for themselves. They are uncomfortable, and they need someone who knows how to do things—you know, the taller, more mobile people who hang around babies making sure they are comfortable (and, hopefully, quiet).

But what about you? You are not a baby, and you know how to do things, like take care of yourself and others. Yet here we are talking about your incredible ability to complain, not that you are even in my category as a complainer. If complaining were an Olympic sport, I would have won a gold medal. I am a lot better now, but there are times when I gripe about something, even something that isn't important.

We complain for the same reason babies grumble: Something isn't right. I've paid attention to why we complain. You complain when something doesn't meet your expectations. Have you ever been to an excellent restaurant with only one location, the kind you need to call weeks ahead to get a reservation? On this night, the restaurant is having a bad time, the kind that causes diners to complain to the manager—and to leave bad reviews on Yelp—because it didn't meet their expectations.

You might also complain when you are uncomfortable, when things are too hot, too cold, or too loud. I've done some research and compiled a list of things that people complain about the most: the weather, traffic, work, lack of time, money, relationship issues, health, customer service, politics, technology, noise, public transportation, internet connectivity (high speed is our birthright), inflation, waiting in line (we're looking at you BMV), sleep, privacy, taxes, education, and environmental issues.

Every person has certain triggers that set off their complaining, but unlike a baby, adults can control their reactions. Yes, you can experience a negative, disappointing experience, like a bad meal or poor customer service without complaining. You are still complaining when after dinner you say, "I am grateful that meal didn't kill me." That's not really a compliment, is it? Write down the top 10 triggers that cause you to complain. Circle any trigger that there is nothing you can do about the source, like weather, traffic, politics, technology, noise, taxes, education, or people with a propensity to complain. If there is nothing you can do about a trigger, then you would do well to recognize that "it is what it is." The weather doesn't cause you to complain, but your beliefs about the weather do. Yes, I agree that it should always be sunny and 74 degrees with a cool breeze coming from over the ocean. You're thinking about San Diego, where I would love to be the weatherman (74, same tomorrow). When the rest of the country chose the president, you voted against them, but spending four years complaining about this person changes nothing. Your experience is made up of your attention and your beliefs. Shift your attention to what is good and positive instead.

The Psychology of Complaining

Some of us complain at times because we want validation—we want others to see things our way. We may also complain to pursue control over others. We may also have been conditioned to complain. Here is what you may not be aware of: the negative effects of complaining. If you don't already have a negative mindset, complaining can cause you to adopt one. Not only does this create pessimism, but it can also cause you to be dissatisfied, failing to appreciate the good and positive things in your life.[1,2] (We'll cover this more in Chapter 5, which is on gratitude.)

You remember the stress we talked about earlier in this book? If you want even more stress, complaining will bring it on. Complaining can harm your mental well-being and bring on anxiety, which can have a negative impact on your physical health.[3] If you are perpetually dissatisfied, you may want to work on experiencing joy, gratitude, and other positive states instead of grumbling all the time.[4]

Complaining can cause you to adopt a victim mentality,[5] giving up your freedom and autonomy. Dispatching the problems that caused you to complain can cause you to grow stronger and develop in positive ways. Growing up, I was not allowed to be a victim. It's better to be the protagonist of the story you are writing.

Complaining can also harm your relationships with your family, friends, and coworkers. You might believe you are venting, but it can cause others to feel they are in a toxic environment. If you are troubled that your frustrations can harm your relationships, know that you don't have to complain about, well ... everything. People who complain find that others avoid them. The social impact can cause people to avoid the person who can't stop bitching all the time. ("Bitching" is a technical term that describes world-class complaining.)

Complaining in the Workplace

You may have had this experience in your work life: There is a leader who rewards people for confessing other people's sins. The person reporting the mistakes of others is positioning themselves with their leader. Having heard the report, the leader starts to complain about these people to their pet. This is how work cultures become toxic.

Other people assign bad intentions to people who have none. For example, a person waiting for a payment to come through might believe that the client didn't pay the invoice because they are trying to steal from the company, or they are holding the payment because they want the float. Much of the time, it turns out that the invoice was buried in their accounting department's email inbox.

Once I was confronted with a salesperson who complained that his boss was wrong about everything, using this as an excuse for his poor results. He could have been a good salesperson, but that would have required him to sell instead of complaining that everything was wrong. In the immortal words of one Steven Tyler of Aerosmith, "The reason a dog has so many friends is because he wags his tail instead of his tongue." This salesperson wagged his tongue. A lot! He poisoned the rest of the sales force. Many of them left the company, and eventually this salesperson left, but only after he created a toxic culture.

Once I witnessed a world-class complainer ruin most of a department by isolating each person, complaining to the people she worked with, working them up until each of them quit the company. After she had finished her work on the department, she left. When she left, the toxicity left with her. Thankfully!

I started working at a large Italian banquet center when I was 13 years old. There were two areas where you could work. The front of the dishwasher had you spraying off the plates. It was gross, and it meant I had to walk the two and half miles home soaking wet after midnight. If you worked the back of the dishwasher, you had to pick up and carry the hot dishes back to the kitchen so they could be replated. I was grateful for the job; I was making money, and the owners fed me prime rib every day. Almost all the dishwashers complained about the water or the heat. I thought these pretty boys who were afraid of getting wet were soft, they had no callouses, and they were afraid of stacking the hot plates. They only stopped complaining when they found another job and quit.

Complaining and Poor Problem-Solving

Here we are back to babies, who are so helpless they can only complain. Complaining can prevent you from dealing with your issues. Instead of using your personal power to deal with the source of your complaints, you share your complaints with others. You can get stuck in a negative loop that lessens your problem-solving skills by complaining and doing nothing. You are better off using this energy to find a solution. It is only my opinion, but complaining seems to create a form of "learned helplessness." You are better off empowering yourself and proactively dealing with the source of your complaints.

One strategy I practice is to deal with the nastiest, most awful task first thing every day. Instead of complaining, I try to solve the problem or challenge. With that out of the way, the rest of the day feels like going downhill.

How to Stop Complaining About Monday

Let's imagine it is Sunday night, and you really don't want to go to work on Monday morning. So there you are, complaining, upset that tomorrow is Monday. Suddenly, there is a knock on the door, and you open it to find the Grim Reaper. He loves his work, and he whispers he is there to take you to the other side, without mentioning exactly which other side you will be spending your eternity in. After a few minutes, you and Grim share a drink or two while watching the NFL Sunday night game. Naturally, Grim is a Patriots fan. You could have guessed that. But now it's the fourth quarter, and even though you tried to overserve Grim, you remember he is already dead.

Man, Monday looks good now, doesn't it!? What would you trade for a couple hundred or thousands of additional Mondays? You would take decades of Mondays with no Saturdays or Sundays as long as you can stay here with the people you love. There are worse things than having to go to work on Monday. It's better than brain surgery, a heart attack, or watching any of the political shows on any of the cable news stations.

But let's get real here. If you are fortunate enough to still have your parents, recognize it is likely they have fewer Mondays left than you do. This means that you have fewer

Mondays with your parent. If you are lucky, you still have your grandparents. They may have even fewer Mondays than your parents. If you want to go and call your people, I will understand. We'll wait for you.

Activity

1. Make a list of those people who matter most to you.
2. Reach out to these people and tell them you love them.

The Stoic Solution

The Stoics had a solution to events or forces that would cause others to complain. If a Stoic was cold and lacking a blanket, they would use the opportunity to test themselves and their stoicism. Some believed that sleeping without a blanket was the gods testing them, reminding them they don't need such comforts to be happy. This reframing of the circumstances is powerful. Epictetus, the Stoic's Stoic, wrote, "There is only one way to happiness and that is to cease worrying about things which are beyond the power of our will."[6] He also wrote, "He is a wise man who does not grieve for the things which he has not but rejoices for those which he has."[7] The ancient Greeks and the Romans who practiced stoicism were on to something.

It's not the event, circumstances, or other people responsible for unhappiness or your complaints. The source of your complaining stems from what you believe about these things. One person can have no emotional response to something that would be processed differently by someone else.

Softness is the opposite of stoicism. The Stoics, especially Marcus Aurelius, held their tongues. We read Marcus Aurelius's *Meditations* because it is perhaps the most profound example of how to live without being negative—and refusing to complain.

It's true you have lived through every negative event, including sitting in the middle seat between two people on a flight from Vermont to Kansas City with a four-year-old child kicking the back of your seat, something that might test the resolve of the most stoic of us. None of these make you a victim unless you choose to process the stimulus in that way. You need not complain about any of these things. Don't worry about the long-term negative events that you experience, as we'll spend an entire chapter on strategies you can use to reframe these negative experiences, even though you will live through the trip.

Steps to Stop Complaining

I don't know what other people do to stop complaining, but I do know what has worked for me. It wasn't easy, but it wasn't all that difficult either. First you have to pay attention to just how much you complain. When you recognize that you complain more than you realized, your awareness might help you to notice you are complaining in your head, that inner dialogue we met some time ago. Before the words leave your mouth, stand down, say nothing. If you don't have something nice to say, don't say anything. There is no reason for you to ruin an experience for others.

Remove Any Offense

Your food is late and cold. You are hungry, and once you get your meal, it wasn't nearly what you expected. But what is worse is that you take offense, as if the waiter and the kitchen were conspiring to offend you. If you replace offense with empathy, you might find yourself wondering why the kitchen is struggling, knowing you can leave and try another restaurant. You can only be offended if you believe that you have somehow been harmed. If a meal disappoints you, there is always Five Guys.

On the first day that I owned a brand new car, the person driving behind me hit my car going about 25 miles an hour. I could see he was on his smartphone as I looked in my rearview mirror. I pulled off the road and made him follow me into the parking lot. I took pictures of his car, my car, and his driver's license. I was livid, but both of us were unharmed. Fortunately, I was past my tendency to complain, or it would have been worse for the other driver.

He begged me not to call the police because he was a professional driver and an accident report could put his job in jeopardy. He apologized and told me that his brother owned a high-end body shop and would repair the car. He called his brother and put him on the phone with me. The driver was negligent, but he had no bad intentions. His brother gave me a car while he repaired mine, making sure it was good as new. It was an accident, not bad intentions.

Recognize When You Have No Control

There are two types of problems you might have. The first type of problem is one that belongs to you. That is an MP (my problem). In this case, you can—and should—do something about whatever might have caused you to complain. The second type of problem is someone else's problem (SEP). If the problem belongs to the president of the United States, remember they worked hard to acquire the worst possible job on Planet Earth, and perhaps, our solar system. All you need to know about things you can't control is to look at how fast presidents age after they are in office. Let the president get old faster while you let things go.

You can spend a lot of time complaining about things that you can't control, spreading negativity far and wide and making other people unhappy. The best thing you can do is accept things as they are and let them go without complaining.

Focus on Solutions

At home and at work, instead of complaining, focus on solutions. While the complaint may allow you to vent your spleen, it also offers an opportunity to do something to make things better. If there is an action you can take instead of complaining, you might find acting reduces your negativity because it causes you to engage your creativity. There is always a viable solution for things you complain about.

One of the best ways to stop complaining is to turn your attention to solving the problem, addressing a challenge, or fixing what is broken. Instead of focusing on what's wrong, you start to figure out what needs to change and how best to make things better.

If we humans are anything, we are infinitely creative. All you need to notice this is to look around at everything that we have created. From airplanes that allow us to fly, to high-rise skyscrapers, to electric cars and rockets that can enter space and return to earth, we have solved very difficult problems. Well, Musk has, anyway.

The door to my office is on the side of the building facing a small lake. There is a wind tunnel that causes the door to swing open. Above the door is an overhang that has been damaged by the door and the wind. Every day for years I struggled with the door, complaining to myself. All that was necessary to improve this was two screws in the overhang to let the door open without getting stuck, something easier than rocket science.

I don't know what your version of the broken door is, but I imagine you have something you complain about without doing anything to make it better.

Finally, remember that you are not a baby. You can help yourself and others, but first you must focus on solutions. Babies cannot be solutions focused, but adults should be if they are going to make a positive impact. You have the power to look at things as they are now and imagine how they can be improved. You have always had the power to change things in your little corner of the world. Instead of complaining, do something to make things better.

Change Your Perspective

Remember that it isn't the event that causes you to complain; it's your belief about the event. I doubt the gods were testing a Stoic's resolve, but treating something like it is a test of your patience is better than complaining and talking yourself into a negative state. The night before I wrote this, I went to dinner with my wife, Cher. The hostess took us to a table next to a large, loud table. Their five young children were noisy and rowdy, and I understood why this was true after their parents started to talk over the children. I made no mention, nor did I complain, as complaining would ruin our dinner. Instead of focusing on the table behind us, I focused on our time together.

My two daughters work at a restaurant with a bar. They make a lot of money, but the clientele could use a bit of an upgrade. The owner requires young women to close late at night. He doesn't provide any security. This is a more serious problem for me. The staff are unhappy, and none of them want to leave their friends behind. Soon they will leave, or I will intervene and explain the owner's responsibility from my view.

Solving Complaining at Work

While I have never visited your workplace, I am certain there a lot of things that could be better. I also know there are a lot of people who complain about how things are now and that they should be better. Many of their complaints are valid, even if they never do anything more than stand around the water cooler complaining to one another. The problem with negativity at work is that negativity is a cancer that spreads by contact. When it metastasizes, you end up with a toxic workplace. You can also have a toxic home if you constantly complain.

It can be difficult to stop complaining at work. Because there are other people and politics in the workplace, you may have to work harder to solve problems. First, there may be an old guard who created a process that no longer works for the business, defending the process they built.

Second, making change might also require spending money, more money than a couple of screws. Despite the challenges of making change, your business and workplace will be improved by you addressing the things you—and your peers—complain about. You may have to build consensus to improve the business and remove one source of complaints before you can tackle another problem.

Another way to improve your workplace is to institute a no-complaining rule, one that would require the person who believes something isn't good enough to draft the solution. If you want leadership to take your complaint seriously, present a solution or a set of potential improvements for their consideration. Then negotiate some change that improves results.

Too many people in the workplace complain without doing anything about the source of the problem, believing changes come from leadership. Most of the time, a great deal of solutions come from the people who deal with the challenges every day. Sell leadership on making things better, including the work environment. Addressing what needs attention and acting can help eliminate the toxic culture that metastasizes when problems are allowed to continue unaddressed.

The Quality of Your Life

The quality of your life is made up of how you process your experiences. It's okay to recognize that something isn't what it should be, but by complaining about it, you are focused on what's wrong, not the solution that could make it better. Complaining comes with too high a price, and it can cost you and others your happiness.

By learning to stop complaining, you reduce your negativity and make room for more positivity. I should warn you that by stopping complaining, you are going to be sensitive to all the complaints you hear from others who, by the way, could use a Negativity Fast of their own. It may bother you, but don't complain about it.

The Science of Complaining

I am a little worried about sharing the science on complaining because it could lead you to believe that it has an upside. It's okay to complain, but not while you are trying to remove negativity. I will make sure you know how to complain when it is necessary.

Let's look at what science can tell us about complaining. First, complaining can cause you to focus your attention on what is negative. This can lead to a more negative outlook, which can lead you to increased stress and anxiety—just the thing we are trying to avoid. Second, when you are complaining about something that is out of your control, it can give you the feeling that you are powerless. The outcome is stress and anxiety. Third, excessive complaining can damage your relationships. Some people, especially people on a Negativity Fast, may avoid you to preserve their own mental well-being.

There are several things you can do if you are complaining excessively. One thing you can do is to exercise. It can reduce your stress and release endorphins, making you feel better. I'll have more to share on this in a future chapter.

Any form of relaxation can help. Whether it is yoga, meditation, or deep breathing exercises, these physical techniques make a difference. One way to feel stressed is to hold your breath, which is why controlling your breathing can have an instant impact on how you feel emotionally and mentally.[8]

Talk to someone you trust, like a family member, a friend, or a therapist. I have had the experience of CBT (cognitive behavioral therapy), and the strategies are practical, and they work wonders on negativity and pessimism. They can reduce complaining.

You can also divert your attention from something negative to something positive. You can change your perspective.

The Upside of Complaining

Complaining is natural to us; it allows us to express our unhappiness, vent our emotions, or achieve an interpersonal goal, sometimes called "intrapsychic goals." Even though complaining can be negative or pessimistic, it is valuable. Here is why: Complaining helps us to identify problems, challenges, and things that need to be improved. When we complain, we are pointing out something that needs attention. The key here is that your complaint should be the beginning of a meaningful process. After you voice your concern, you need to do something about it. This could be focusing on how to create positive change or deciding that the complaint isn't all that important and letting it go. Complaining can be positive if it is a first step. The problem occurs when complaining doesn't lead to anything.

Even though people avoid complainers, occasional complaints can also improve relationships. If we are anything, we are complicated. Part of this strategy seems to cause people to trust and value the person they share with. Nothing bonds people together more than having to deal with problems.

While complaining can cause stress and anxiety, it can also help us cope with stress. Complaining is one way to express our negative feelings.

One of the intrapsychic goals is that it makes the person feel better about themselves. It's also important to know that some people complain to manipulate and control other people.

Here are four rules that will help you complain without being negative:

1. **Be specific.** Don't generalize. Explain your complaint so others understand. When you say, "Everything here is terrible," that is too broad. First, you're exaggerating, and second, you can't solve everything. Try this instead: "We don't have the support we need to take care of clients. We need another person."

2. **Focus on problems.** This one can be a little more difficult. You should focus on the problem and not the person. You may find that the person isn't to blame; the process is. But if it turns out to be this person's fault, treat them like you would want your children to be treated should they struggle.

3. **Respect other people's views or opinions.** Ask them to share their perspective. You may have a little conflict around something you or others are complaining about. You may be missing some information, or maybe someone else is missing it. Be patient and professional and ask that party to explain what's going on, what they have tried, and what might work. If you want people to listen to your perspective, listen to theirs.

4. **Be prepared to negotiate or compromise.** You may not always get the solution you want. You may have to split the difference, trading support for you and another party to both get what you want. Compromise and diplomacy will make you more successful.

Please work to stop complaining as we work our way to the Negativity Fast. But if you complain, I will hold my tongue and make no complaint. Maybe the complaint needs to be surfaced.

5

The Awesome Power of Gratitude

Gratitude and Attitude

Practicing gratitude has several proven benefits, including many psychological advantages like happiness, well-being, reduced depression and anxiety, greater self-esteem, and an increased ability to deal with stress.[1] Gratitude also can help with your health through better sleep, lower blood pressure, a stronger immune system, and reduced chronic pain and inflammation.[2,3] And there are additional positive social outcomes like building stronger bonds and relationships, encouraging forgiveness (something we all need), and reducing negative emotions like anger.[4]

Gratitude can help you be more positive and less negative. But our negativity bias has us looking for what is wrong instead of what is right. In September 2021, the Global Rich List suggested that $32,400 would find you in the top 1% in the world. The people who lack almost everything you have would trade places with you in a millisecond, but I suspect that having traded places, they would still experience a negativity bias over time. One way to stop complaining is by practicing gratitude.

To describe the nature of our world, Taoists use the concept of yin and yang, which describes opposite but interconnected forces. Yin is the receptive element, and yang is the active principle. You would never know warmth without exposure to the cold, and you wouldn't know up without knowing down. Taoists see these opposites as two sides of one idea. We can describe gratitude as the other side of complaining.

Gratitude means being thankful for the positives in your life. But for this to be true, you must value those good things when they show up, which is every day—if you are looking for them. To be truly grateful, you must recognize both goodness as well as the source of the good things you have, like your health, your family, a roof over your head, enough food, and your friends. There are people who lack the things we take for granted, and we need to be grateful for what we have.

Were you to try to count your blessings, your inventory would be difficult to calculate. But here are some ideas about what people say they are grateful for: health, family (including Uncle Enrico, the conspiracy theorist), friends, nature, opportunities, a home, food, love, emotional support, financial stability, freedom, and safety. This list is a good start on what you could be grateful for, but there are surely others, like all dogs, a small number of cats, bookstores, music, movies, art, college football, or the fact that you are here at this time. You know you could have been born in a far more difficult time, like during the Great Depression or World War II.

Often we allow the weapon of mass distractions (the smartphone) to turn our attention to what we don't have. When we acquire what the phone shows us, it brings us little joy. Let's be honest about the cardboard boxes that show up on your front porch every day. Whatever is in that box isn't likely to make you happy or fulfilled. Recently I asked our delivery guy if my house receives the most boxes in the neighborhood. (I was considering buying a forklift to manage them more easily.) He said we aren't anywhere near the top when it comes to deliveries. One of our neighbors gets so many packages, he feels he needs to check on them if a couple of days go by and they haven't had any deliveries. I'm sorry to tell those who enjoy their retail therapy that the stuff we bring into our lives does nothing to reduce our negativity. There is a concept called hedonic adaptation that suggests that after buying something, you go back to your baseline in a short period of time.[5] You know that fancy car your bought, the one that felt great? In a few months, it's just a car. A lot of things we own eventually own us. Let me prove this claim. If you have an iPhone, it requires you to pick it up and carry it with you everywhere. Data from a consumer insights agency says the average user engages with their phone 76 separate times a day. Heavy users averaged 132 sessions a day.[6]

I challenge you to be grateful for everything good in your life. This is a choice you can make, and one that will improve your life far more than anything that comes in a box. Many with this affliction don't recognize that they are blessed, and some don't know they are ungrateful (hello, teenagers!). At times we can all fail to be grateful, even when we have much to be thankful for.

In my first book, which is for salespeople, I recommend they keep a gratitude journal because selling comes with losses. Some salespeople believe their prospects are rejecting them personally, even though this is not true. In sales and any other endeavor, you tend to do better by being positive, optimistic, future-oriented, and empowered. This helps to lessen the tendency to take the role of victim.

How to Start Practicing Gratitude

One way to start a gratitude practice is to take an inventory of all things for which you should be grateful. Include every good thing you have now and good things you have had in the past, including the experiences you've had throughout your life. It is sometimes easier to make a list, as it challenges your mind to fill in the blanks. This list should include the people who have had a profound impact on your life. Our negativity bias has us constantly looking for what is wrong. An inventory of what you are grateful for can help you recognize what you have that is positive and worth being grateful for. Because we tend to take things for granted, it's doubtful that you recall all the things you should be grateful for. When you make this list, don't give up too quickly; much more than you initially imagine will come to mind when you work on your list. Hint: Start with people and experiences, because these things avoid hedonistic adaptation.

Another way to begin practicing gratitude is to start a gratitude journal. This is as simple as it sounds: Dedicate time each day to reflect on the past 24 hours and write down anything you feel thankful for. I had a tough time adopting this practice until I started making time to write in the morning.

Some people prefer a paper journal while others prefer a digital format. My best advice is to select a journal that you will enjoy writing in, even if it's something you need to pay for, whether it's a notebook or a digital journal like the Day One app. You can even keep it simple by typing into a Google Doc or a Microsoft Word document. I use software called Obsidian.md because the files are on my computer and not in the cloud. I also like to write in plain text, so I can focus on the writing without formatting.

The trick is to write something every day, no matter how small. You can always find something to appreciate. For example, imagine that you are delighted that two finches built a nest in the light on your front porch, so you write down the experience. (If you are Cher, you hang a feeder on the tree out front to make them feel as comfortable and welcome as possible.) If these birds come back every spring, you may be excited as you document the same event in your gratitude journal several years in a row, and this can serve as a seasonal reminder of the wonders of the natural world.

One of the challenges of keeping a gratitude journal is repeating similar entries, even though it is more than okay to repeat yourself. While some people may feel the same enjoyment seeing local birds return, others may feel less excited each year. It can be even more difficult to feel grateful for smaller events that happen frequently. For example, if you go out to dinner with some friends and have a lovely time, you might make an entry in your gratitude journal. But you might get bored making similar entries over and over. If you feel out of ideas or bored of writing about the same things, the following sections will help you get unstuck.

Honing Your Focus

One of the easiest ways to get started with a gratitude journal is by writing about the people you love, your spouse or significant other, your children, or other members of your family. You're likely to write about these people regularly, so it's important to keep things fresh.

One way to do this is to go from the general to the specific. So, you love your spouse and your children. What is it about each of them that you are grateful for? You can focus on specific character traits or something they recently did that made you particularly proud, thankful, or happy. By going from a general sense of gratitude to specific details, you can improve your journaling and improve your gratitude. It also helps you see everyday experiences with fresh eyes, which helps increase your appreciation.

Seligman's Three Blessings

One of my favorite biographies is *The Hope Circuit: A Psychologist's Journey from Helpless to Optimism* by Martin E.P. Seligman, the father of positive psychology. In the book, Seligman provides a history of one of the major changes in psychology. When Seligman started his work in psychology, his main objective was figuring out how to eliminate misery. However, instead of that, he refocused his research on what makes life worth living, a shift that led to his development of positive psychology.[7]

Seligman recommends an activity called Three Blessings. You write down three successes or good things from the day, including why they went well. Seligman recommends you keep this up for a week to benefit from a shift in your mindset, but you can make it an ongoing part of your daily routine.

Seligman examined data from studies that relied on double-blind placebo controls to determine the efficacy of psychotherapy and medication in patients with depression. Then he compared those results to people who practiced the Three Blessings exercise. He found that, on its own, the Three Blessings "reliably lowered depression and raised life satisfaction for as long as six months." He continues, "These results were comparable, perhaps superior to the effect of medication and psychotherapy in severe depression."[8]

I am not a psychologist, but I do believe that if you allow your negativity bias to focus on what is wrong, you will find plenty of reasons to be more negative than positive. The inverse also feels true. If you look for what is good, it seems you can override your negativity bias by being grateful for the good things in your life.

I have done the Three Blessings practice and found it to be so powerful that I encouraged my employees to adopt it. At one of my companies everyone shares their Three Blessings in a Google Chat. Every day, people comment and use emojis to support each other's blessings. The business is one where a lot of things go wrong. I expected this to go on for a couple weeks, but each day, people come back and recount there Three Blessings. In our meetings, there is less complaining and more positivity

This is a simple but profound exercise. If it can reduce depression, it is surely powerful enough to temper your negativity. In some ways, I think this is an upgrade to a gratitude journal. Because you are recounting the three things that went well during your day, it isn't so repetitive. You can also journal your interactions with the people you love. Taking a page from Seligman, you can write a Three Blessing entry and recount what went well for you and why. Take your time and reflect on the entry you are journaling. Put yourself in the emotional space and recount why it made you feel good. You might also write your personal experiences. Sometimes it's easier to keep up this practice if you occasionally go back and read earlier entries.

Look in Unlikely Places

I don't believe you can truly be grateful unless you are thankful for everything in your life, even the negative events. My father left my family when I was seven years old, one of my many young traumas. My mother refused to allow me to carry any hate in my heart, saving me from carrying something so heavy. With no positive male role model, at 12 years old I felt liberated to do whatever I wanted whenever I wanted. The upside is that even though I was reckless, my teenage years were quite an adventure.

My mom tried to instill her values in me. I was a horrible little monster, but over time she won, and I ended up with her honesty, charity, and sense of duty. I am grateful for her influence. I apologize to her constantly for being such a difficult kid, reminding her of how grateful I am for her example.

I have a journal entry of 10 negative events and why I am grateful for each one. I don't see them as entirely negative. They were all some part of my path. I could easily write another 20 entries about the positivity I earned going through difficult experiences. These types of entries follow a pattern that helps me reframe my thinking: *If [this negative event] hadn't happened, [this positive outcome] would not have occurred.*

Negative events shaped your path and your person in some positive way. Psychologist Carl Jung called this "shadow work," where you look directly at the parts of you that you are not proud of. By shining a light on your shadow, you can fully integrate negative aspects of your life back into yourself in a positive way. If you are depressed or suffering, you should avoid this work unless you are working with a professional. This process is mental and spiritual, and it can cause an emotional response.

Using a Grievance Journal

You likely knew what a gratitude journal was before picking up this book, but you may not have heard of a grievance journal. A grievance journal is the opposite of the gratitude journal, giving you a place to express thoughts and feelings like "I feel like my boss doesn't respect my opinion." If something is on your mind and causing negativity or negative feelings, you write it in your journal. The best practice here is starting the sentence with the word "I" followed by how you feel. Here we are returning to Albert Ellis's ABC (Chapter 3) by dealing with our feelings instead of the activating event or our beliefs. The real value of this journal is that it allows you consider your feelings and emotions with objectivity. For example, there is a difference between saying, "I feel like my boss has it in for me" and "My boss has it in for me." Ellis's ABC helps us reorient to understand that distinction. Not everything you feel is true, but it's also not necessarily untrue.

Objectivity allows you to examine your feelings from an outside perspective. Like most of the strategies in this book, being able to do this will help you manage your emotions, reduce your negativity, and improve your mental health. You can also gain an emotional distance from your feelings by labeling them. Using "I" to start your journal entry, you write something like, "I notice that I am feeling angry." This practice is close to mindfulness.

If you happen to see certain patterns, whether people, events, or feelings, you may want to think about making changes that would eliminate these sources of negativity. You can also use your grievance journal to write what you might do to solve your problems. As Jim Rohn would say, "If you don't like how things are, change it! You are not a tree." For example, there is a person who takes advantage of you due to their role. This pattern will continue until you decide to politely and professionally push back and set boundaries or leave for a place where you will be treated better. This is how you use your personal power. Or maybe the environment you find yourself in has become so toxic it is time to escape from the negativity and find a more positive space. In nature, there are two types of hierarchies: a dominator hierarchy and a growth hierarchy. You would do well to leave a dominator hierarchy and find your way to a growth hierarchy, where you will be supported.

One mistake people make with a grievance journal is writing down names and events in a way that encourages scorekeeping with people. That approach can undermine objectivity and reinforce the idea that some people are adversaries. The goal of documenting grievances is to focus on the positive aspects of the situation. For example, you might have a disagreement with a colleague, but the positive outcome could be that you learned how to have a more productive relationship with them in the future.

Even situations that seem entirely negative can offer hidden benefits. Imagine you get sick during a highly anticipated vacation, so you miss out on most of the activities you had been looking forward to. Acknowledge your disappointment and then, instead of dwelling on it, try to find some positive aspect of the situation, no matter how slim that might be. For instance, maybe the timing would have been worse if you had gotten sick during an upcoming business trip. Or perhaps you could appreciate being able to rest and recuperate in a beautiful place where you don't have to worry about daily household chores. You want to avoid keeping score because that is certain to make you negative and will not help you become more positive. The more you focus on difficult people and events, the more you entrench yourself in negativity. You use the grievance journal to create distance, not to keep track and review every offense.

Building a Fire Board

I believe I may have created the idea of the Fire Board. At one point I had an overwhelming number of problems that needed my attention, although nothing was actually on fire. I listed them in order of importance and titled it "Fire Board." That gave me a sense of control so I could start to put out the many fires.

You know how sometimes your problems start to stack one on top of another until you are overwhelmed? You can objectify your problems by making a list, moving these problems out of your body and mind and onto a piece of paper, where you can create distance. Before you go to sleep, make a list of the things about which there is nothing you can do. Draw a line through each one of the problems that you can't solve. Then make a list of problems that you can do something about and write down the first action you can take after you get a good night's sleep. This exercise can allow you to sleep because you have already started working on what needs your attention and you have a plan to deal with what you can control or influence upon waking up.

As you look at the list, you are going to find two different types of problems. Some portion of these problems are not in your control, like losing your largest client because they decided to move their headquarters out of your city or state without giving you any notice. Try as you may, other than acquiring another client, there is nothing you can do about this problem. Because this event is out of your control, you can let go of that problem and start trying to replace this unfaithful client.

Another problem on your list is that you have too much work to be able to complete an important project.

This could be a problem because you have a tough time saying no, because you want to be helpful, or because you haven't established boundaries and you tend to overextend yourself. This too belongs on your Fire Board. Even though you accepted too many projects, this is in your control. You can ask for help, renegotiate timelines, or find someone who can take over one or more of your projects.

You might also have personal challenges that show up on your Fire Board, like a child struggling in school or a leaky roof. You can't control these events or situations, but you can do something about them. One by one, you put out the fires, resolving them.

There are things that are completely out of your control, like genetic predispositions, the actions of others, the rate of change in our environment, technological advances that displace jobs, aging and mortality, natural disasters, global wars, and, as you might remember, global pandemics.

Capturing your problems on paper can help you feel that you have greater control. It is empowering to let go of things that are completely out of your control or influence, and it is helpful to know there is something you can do about your problems, if you don't mistake things that you can't control for things you can control.

The Power of Saying Thank You

There are good reasons to say thank you, outside of making others know you appreciate what they have done for you, even though this a good enough reason by itself. Expressing thanks takes little time or effort, and you'll find opportunities to do so every day. Look for them, no matter how small or large. It's not only good for the person you are thanking, but it is also good for you.

A Change in Your Perspective

When you express your gratitude by saying thank you, you can shift from negative to positive, focusing on what you appreciate. It's sometimes difficult to believe these simple, practical strategies can reduce negativity and create greater positivity.[9] Yet these practices are not generally known, let alone taught in school, something that might help children build a set of habits that would help them thrive in our current environment of accelerating, constant disruptive change.

Improving Your Mental Health

There is research showing gratitude is linked to better mental health by reducing stress, anxiety, high blood pressure, and even depression. When you are grateful even in a negative situation, you have an easier time managing your emotional states.[10] This is a decision, a choice you make that can help you remove negativity. If we need anything right now, it is a general improvement in our mental health and well-being.

Building Better Relationships

After money problems and infidelity, I believe a top reason that marriages fall apart is a single question: "What's for dinner?" No one wants to answer that question seven days a week—or be the only one in the household who is expected to answer that question. By asking about dinner, you can create an obligation without meaning to. Cher makes dinner for us most nights. I say thank you after every meal because I appreciate her effort to take care of me. This is not only gratitude, but also a form of respect, and it can build a stronger relationship. There are countless opportunities to say thank you. Should you want, you could suggest a restaurant or pick up something on your way home, in which case you will get the thank you—and avoid having a lawyer serve you with papers.

Gratitude Creates a Positive Environment

Your gratitude promotes positivity and lessens negativity. Using this practice at work—where there may be conflict with your peers, your clients, and the companies that supply you with whatever you company buys from them—can help prevent or improve a toxic environment.

Small Things Are Big Things

Last week, I went to lunch with Cher. I forgot my phone at home, maybe because my subconscious mind finds it boring after I removed all social media platforms. Lunch was better without a phone, no text messages or email or other notifications. A few days later I left the house without the phone again. I didn't miss it.

Seemingly small things are the big things, and the big things are often the small things. Getting this backward can reduce the quality of your life, your health, and your life expectancy.

I have followed the Harvard Study since it was managed by George Valiant, who picked up the study in 1972. This study has been being pursued since 1938. The gist of the results is that the key to a happy, fulfilling life is strong social connections.[11] To follow the science of happiness and a good life is to have close, supportive relationships with your family and your friends. It makes you happier and healthier, and it can help you live longer. Those who are isolated are less happy, less healthy, and have shorter lives.

The number of relationships isn't as important as the quality. These relationships seem to protect our health and lower our stress. The study suggests that loneliness is the equivalent of smoking 15 cigarettes a day. Purpose gives us meaning and direction. One other factor from this study shows that our ability to bounce back from adversity is critically important to our happiness.

You may not have known about the Harvard Study, but most of us don't follow the conclusions as well as we might.

How We Live Poorly

In a world that is becoming more transactional when it comes to relationships, we are off course. Our modern life fails in the realm of relationships and how we live.

My grandmother knew her neighbors. They shared what they baked, and three of her four neighbors had a key to her house, and she had keys to theirs. They looked after each other's kids and spent time outside talking to each other. I doubt your neighbors have the code to open your garage or your front door. Instead, we have doorbells that record the people who walk up our driveways, sharing them on Next Door.

When we are not in front of the television watching Netflix, we are staring into the small screen of infinite scrolling. Looking at images on Instagram, following political arguments on Twitter, or watching videos on TikTok and YouTube, as if this a good use of our 4,108 weeks. Most people pick up their iPhone more frequently than a mother picks up a newborn baby. How's that for priorities?

The promise of technology was a better life, but for all it brings us, it comes with a dark side. We are distracted. We are not present for each other. We are too busy to do the things that lead to a good life. Now we are told we should find our way to a metaverse designed to remove us from real life and enter a cartoon life with strangers who are there to convert you into a customer in a world that is nowhere near as rich an experience as the world we live in now.

The reason that relationships are critical to our happiness is because we need each other. We need to belong. We need others, family, and friends. We need to care for each other. This is our nature, and you show your gratitude to God or the Universe by spending your time living the good life.

The Science of Gratitude

An article titled "The Theories and Effect of Gratitude: A System Review" by Zixi Zeng focuses on gratitude and its ability to reduce negativity and its positive outcomes. The paper suggests that gratitude is a positive emotion that can increase happiness, improve your satisfaction with your life, and build resilience. It reduces our negativity by shifting our focus to the positive things in our lives and away from negative experiences. It can also improve our relationships, building stronger bonds with others.[12] One way to build your gratitude is to keep a gratitude journal, cultivate mindfulness practices, and express gratitude for others.

A study by Emmons and McCullough found that keeping a gratitude journal for 10 weeks caused the participants to feel happier, more optimistic, and more grateful. They also had fewer symptoms of anxiety or depression.[13] A study by Froh and Bono found that grateful people were more likely to help others and less likely to gossip or complain.[14]

Here is a list of positive outcomes that come from gratitude:

- Happiness
- Improved sleep
- Reduced stress
- Increased optimism
- Increased resilience
- Stronger relationships
- Increased generosity
- Increased self-esteem
- Improved physical health.

Do This Now

- **Start a gratitude journal.** Pick up a journal or a notebook and start writing. You don't need to write a long entry. Just write what you are grateful for right now. If you are stuck, use Seligman's Three Blessings.
- **Practice mindful appreciation.** There are more than enough opportunities to appreciate some common courtesy or someone going out of their way to help you. Start noticing what you should appreciate.
- **Express gratitude to others.** Say thank you every time you have an opportunity. This is a good practice, as it builds better bonds and relationships. It also helps you with your well-being.

(Continued)

(*Continued*)

- **Focus on what's good in your life.** The way to beat back your negativity bias is to focus on what is good. My son often greets me by saying, "What's good?"
- **Most of all, appreciate the people who are important to you.** There is nothing more important than the people in your life.

6

Reframing Negative Events

Why a Cancer Diagnosis Is the Best Thing That Ever Happened to Me

In late October 1992, I came to after being restrained in a van. The two men in the van were hard for me to understand. I knew I had to escape, and fast, before something bad happened to me. Unable to break the cuffs holding me in place, I argued that I had done nothing wrong and that they had no right to take me against my will.

It turned out they were paramedics, and I was in the back of an ambulance. One of the paramedics, who arrived after my landlord called 911, tried to explain that I had just suffered a grand mal seizure. After having a seizure, one thing I learned is I was the only person unaware of what had happened. Without knowing what I was saying, I told the two people preventing me from leaving the ambulance that I knew the laws of California and that they had to let me out. To be sure, I knew nothing of the laws in California or any state. I had no idea what I was saying.

After repeating myself over and over, one nice paramedic told me I was right, in California they must release you. I climbed out of the ambulance and walked into my apartment. My captors followed me into my small Brentwood apartment, where I lived alone. The second paramedic cornered me in my kitchen and asked me what time I got home, and I answered 5:30. It was after 6:15. He asked me where I had been during that time. I had lost 45 minutes after leaving rush hour on the 405 Freeway.

My brain was not working well. My neighbor noticed something was going on and offered to drive me to the UCLA Medical Center. Instead of going with professional medical caregivers, I found my way to the hospital in my neighbor's 1980s Chevy Chevette with the ambulance following us. I was rushed into a CT scan, and after a few minutes, I was inside an MRI. If you have a CT scan and they decide to follow up with an MRI, you are in trouble.

Sometime later, a neurosurgeon entered my room and showed me the giant spot on the front right temporal lobe. He told me I had cancer, and they would need to remove the front right lobe to protect the left lobe. I complained that I was not interested in a lobotomy. He countered, "It wouldn't be a lobotomy. It would only be a lobectomy, as I would only lose half of my brain. I wasn't sure I had enough to spare. I asked the doctor if I could have "not cancer," communicating the idea as well as I could under the circumstances.

He told me I might have another condition called an AVM (arteriovenous malformation) noting that it would be the largest they had ever seen. The next morning, I had a procedure where a tube was entered into my femoral artery and guided up to by brain, where dye was inserted into the arteries and veins in my skull to discern the dark spot on the MRI. I was relieved to discover I had an AVM, which isn't great, unless you compare it to brain cancer.

I called my parents to inform them that I was at the hospital and that I had a serious problem. I flew back to Columbus, Ohio, and was referred to consult with Dr. John Tew, the world's leading neurosurgeon specializing in AVMs, who had a practice in Cincinnati. A week later, I had two surgeries. The first surgery was done to close the arteries and veins using an epoxy, and I was mostly awake for the nine-hour surgery. The next day, Dr. Tew and his team removed the AVM and a large piece of bruised brain that might cause seizures in the future. Dr. Tew told me only after the surgery that I had lost part of my brain. After leaving the hospital, I was angry.

It may have been because I had my skull opened, or woke up without a piece of my brain, or the anti-seizure drugs they gave me, but I was angry. It was likely a combination of these and other factors—and the feeling lingered. One memory I am not proud of is getting out of my car and chasing a man after he blocked me from turning into a parking lot.

What I Learned from Two Brain Surgeries

I started talking when I was nine months old and could read before I was four years old. From the minute I learned to read, I have been an avid reader, reading a book a week. I had no interest in graduating high school, skipping as many classes as I could, mostly to work washing dishes. If it wasn't for my mother threatening to sit next to me in every class, I would have dropped out.

After losing a piece of my brain, I overcompensated for the loss by going to college when I was 26. I graduated summa cum laude with a 3.93 grade point average and 4.0 in my major, political science, and my minor, English literature. It was easy for me because I had already quit alcohol and was no longer a teenager. Between my high GPA and high LSAT score, I won the dean's academic scholarship to law school, choosing not to take the bar after recognizing that lawyers aren't a happy lot. A few years later, I attended the Owner/President Management program at Harvard Business School, the last step in my nine years of education. This was a complete overreaction to losing part of my brain, my version of Dorothy's Scarecrow. That was nine years of education. Before that, I was playing rock 'n' roll.

I gave up playing rock 'n' roll when grunge replaced hair metal. Hair metal was fun, but grunge was negative, so much so that, at least in part, it led to the losses of Kurt Cobain (Nirvana), Layne Staley (Alice In Chains), Scott Weiland (Stone Temple Pilots), Chris Cornell (Soundgarden), and Chester Bennington (Linkin Park). Music had changed—it was no longer a party; it was dark and negative.

After my surgeries, I was better able to recognize the value of my relationships. I had believed that I would never live to see 25 (which almost happened), but now I was grateful for more time—good, bad, or ugly. At a big sales conference, I gave a short preview of the concepts in this book, mentioning that people who live though cancer say it's the best thing that ever happened to them. Their trauma changes them in positive ways. They experience a perspective change. When I left the stage, several people in the audience stopped me to tell me it was true; they were improved through their trauma, each grateful for something awful.

In a paper titled "Posttraumatic Growth: Conceptual Foundations and Empirical Evidence" by Richard G. Tedeschi and Lawrence G. Calhoun of the University of North Carolina at Charlotte, there are a few things to learn about trauma and why some grow from negative events and outcomes. Using a 21-item scale to measure post-traumatic growth, five factors seem present: "greater appreciation of life, warmer, more intimate relationships with others, a greater sense of personal strength, recognition of new possibilities for one's life, and spatial development."[1]

There are two personalities that may lead to people to grow after trauma: people who are extroverts and open to different experiences, and "[a]ctivity, positive emotions, and openness to feelings are the three characteristics most strongly related to posttraumatic growth." I was fortunate to be an extrovert, one with a greater appreciation of life.

Freud and Adler

A disclosure is necessary here. Nothing minimizes the trauma you may have experienced during your life. When you were harmed in some way, you experienced the trauma and pain that followed. It can take time for your perspective to change, and as far as I can tell, there isn't a way to speed up the process. The choice we make after trauma has a large impact on the quality of our lives and how we live them. To help you recognize the choices available to you, we need to look to a couple of psychoanalysts to help us understand our choice about how we process our traumas.

You may be familiar with Sigmund Freud. You may not, however, be aware of another psychoanalyst named Alfred Adler, who was Freud's contemporary. Freud and Adler had different ideas about trauma. Freud believed your traumas were permanent and the source of your unhappiness. It is true that some people create a narrative to justify their current state, or their limitations, based on their trauma. This concept is called etiology, and it stands for the cause of the disease.[2] I'm sure you have a relative who uses some past experience to explain why they can't do something you are certain they could do easily. (If I had to guess, it's one of your cousins on your father's side.)

Adler, on the other hand, would tell you that no single negative experience can cause you to fail or ensure you succeed in the future. You and I create the meaning of the trauma to help us explain ourselves. This concept is called teleologic. Adler believed life is hard, and you can change.[3]

I have a large scar that starts at the top of my forehead and ends behind my right ear. The scar is like a tattoo with a better story and a positive impact. During a post-surgery follow-up visit with Dr. Sigmund, my neurologist, he provided me with a form I needed to complete. At the top of the form were two options. I could check the first box, allowing me to collect disability for the rest of my life. Checking the second box would mean my bills would be paid for three months, at which time I would have exhausted my temporary disability. I asked Dr. Sigmund if I was somehow disabled. His answer stuck with me from the minute the words escaped his lips. He said, "You are disabled if you believe you are." I checked the second box, certain I was not disabled.

The traumas we experience can only limit us when we invest negative meaning into these events, telling and retelling the story. Your story or my story can be one of surviving and overcoming, or it can be one we tell ourselves to explain why we are something less after trauma. One way to be less negative is to reframe your negative events and traumas.

There is a story about motivational speakers. While sitting in the audience watching a speaker tell their story about losing their business, their spouse leaving them, their dog dying, and finding out they have cancer, those watching whisper, "Why do all the good things happen to them?"

Two Ls: Losses or Lessons

Let's call an event that harms you a "loss." You can live with your loss without it improving your life and your future. You can also decide to refuse to accept the "loss," by turning it into a lesson. You are still here, and you have time in front of you, and you are leaving the event with a lesson, even if you paid too much to learn it. If you wonder why your parents told you not to do something, it's because they already knew how the story would end. You may wonder how your parents knew to tell you not to do things that might harm you. My mom used to ask me, "If everyone jumped off a cliff, would you do it too?" I told tell her I would wait until the bodies piled up high enough to break my fall. After several negative events, I acquired a sixth sense that caused me to leave before something bad happened. The lessons that stick are the ones that come at a cost.

When I was a junior in high school, I came home to see my sister's boyfriend roughing her up, pushing her into his car. I ran across the front yard and hit him in the face as hard as I could. I weighed 125 pounds, and Mark, the boyfriend, was 225 pounds, the starting quarterback of the football team, and a heavyweight wrestler. If you have never been in a fight, you might not know that your mouth tastes like copper as you experience an adrenaline drop. Fights, thankfully, last just a couple of minutes. When Mark hit me, my head hit the curb, causing a concussion. He busted my eye and my lips. I ended up chasing him to his car and running after him as he left my neighborhood. When I walked into my house, I hit the wall and broke my pinky finger. (I'm certain that taught him a lesson.) I have never been interested in physical violence, but I have a dozen stories where I was not given a choice. I learned that just fighting back was enough to cause people to avoid a second fight.

You can reframe your losses into lessons, making a negative into a positive. If you learned something from a trauma or a loss, the lesson means you gained something positive from something negative. Writing what you learned from a negative event can help you realize how you are improved, stronger, and able to deal with greater challenges. Your negative experiences provide an education, if you get past the negative experience and learn something that may improve your future.

Most of the time, you need only touch the stove once to learn not to touch fire; that lesson is learned without being repeated. There is always a lesson in a loss that can change your perspective and make you wiser if you reframe it.

Post-Traumatic Growth Syndrome

Nassim Nicholas Taleb is the author of five books. His best is titled *Antifragile: Things That Gain from Disorder*. Taleb was a financial trader, and he knows you can't time the market. To make sure he is antifragile, he always has a put (a bet that at some time, there will be large event that causes the market to fall precipitously).

As a trader, Taleb was responsible for ensuring his wealthy clients stayed wealthy when markets turned down. Had you given Taleb the $25 million dollars you need to have his hedge fund manage your money, the pandemic no one expected would have returned you an increase greater than 4,000%. One of his more important contributions is the concept of antifragility, as there was only fragility before Taleb discovered its opposite. The bet against the market makes him antifragile, as he gains from a negative event.

To explain this concept of antifragility, Taleb describes three states: (1) fragile, (2) robust, and (3) antifragile. Something fragile will break when it is harmed, like a box full of glass being dropped off the back of a truck. Something that is robust or resilient isn't harmed, but neither is it improved, like a box of paper towels being dropped off that same truck.

Which brings us to the antifragile. When you harm something that is antifragile, you make it stronger.[4]

Up until this point in your life, you may have wanted to be resilient, like the mythical phoenix, who rises from the ashes after being harmed. But being antifragile means you are better after being harmed. Instead of being the phoenix, you are the mythical hydra. When you cut off one of the hydra's heads, two more grow in its place. Freud would have thought you fragile, Adler would find you to be robust, but the better state is antifragile, getting stronger from what harms you.

Another philosopher, one Friedrich Nietzsche, would tell you "that which does not kill you makes you stronger."[5] Khalil Gibran would counsel that "Out of our suffering have emerged the strongest souls. The most massive characters are seared with scars."[6] It's impossible to write a book of negativity without bumping into the Stoics, like Marcus Aurelius, who wrote a couple thousand years ago: "You have power over your mind—not outside events. Realize this, and you will find strength."[7]

How to Become a Hydra

We believe that stress is bad for us, but that isn't exactly true. Stress can be harmful to your health and your mental health. But there is another kind of stress called eustress. This stress is moderate or normal psychological stress, interpreted as being beneficial. You may feel this eustress when you are dealing with a challenge you believe you can handle. This is a positive stress. One benefit of being a hydra is that you interpret negative events as having a positive outcome for you. Your losses are lessons. What harms you makes you stronger, if you reframe the trauma that Adler addressed, suggesting that nothing in your past can harm your future.

People often say that bad things happen to good people. But the truth is that bad things happen to everyone, some more than others. The way to deal with the bad things that happen is to reframe them, making them a positive. It may take time and distance to recognize the upside of the negative event and gain an awareness of how you are improved, and you may need to gain some distance to do this and be able to identify and process the negative event.

You may know someone who was given everything. They never had to struggle in any meaningful way, and they were spoiled. Because they were never required to do anything on their own, they have a certain weakness. They lack the competence that you would expect. This is because they have not been exposed to "hormesis," a word coined by pharmacologists. Hormesis occurs when a small dose of a harmful substance is beneficial for you.

You know how you go to the gym to lift heavy weights? What you are doing is tearing your muscles a little, and by doing so, your muscles become stronger and bigger, causing people to ask if you have a license to carry those big guns of yours, brocephis. Congratulations, now you are all swole, but you can't scratch your back without backing up to a doorway to deal with an itch, thanks to hormesis.

Adversity and Traumatic Growth Syndrome

Research suggests that close to 80% of people will experience some form of traumatic event in their lifetime. Some of us may experience more than one. According to Maurer and Daukantaite, trauma can "shatter one's assumptions of the world forcing one to reckon with a disruption of their belief system."[8]

The concept of growth after adversity is based on our inherent motivation toward greater well-being. We cope with the adversity, or we grow from it. We take one path by holding on to their previous assumptions "returning to the level prior to the trauma." This is what we call resilience. It is also possible to let adversity or trauma alter your worldview.[9]

When we process the information as positive, we rebuild our assumptions and incorporate the trauma, finding new meaning or a positive outcome. This can provide us with a "greater appreciation of life," a greater sense of gratitude, a greater connection with one's true values, feeling of authenticity, or a deeper sense of connection with other people."[10]

Yet when one accommodates the information in a positive way, this means that one rebuilds one's assumptive world, incorporating the trauma information, but being able to find a new meaning or positive angle with this change in one's life. Such changes might entail greater appreciation of life, a greater sense of gratitude, greater connection with one's true values, feelings of authenticity, or a deepened sense of connection with other people.[11]

In the movie *Conan the Barbarian*, Arnold Schwarzenegger plays Conan. At the beginning of the movie, a young Conan and his peers are kidnapped by the bad guys. They are required to push a giant wheel continuously. A few minutes into the movie we see a now-giant Conan turning the wheel by himself. His captors gave him the trauma and adversity that would later allow him to take revenge. (Please don't watch the movie, but if you do, don't blame me.)

In an article titled "Biological Correlates of Post-Traumatic Growth (PTG): A Literature Review," Dell'Osso and colleagues focus on reframing negative events to be post-traumatic growth syndrome.[12] They describe this process as reflecting on experiences to find meaning in them.

Reframing is the ability to shift the way you look at a negative event to view it as positive, or resulting in certain benefits. To do this, one must look for meaning in the negative experience and recognize an opportunity for growth. For example, someone who experienced trauma may appreciate their life, find a new purpose, or focus on their relationships.

This is the first paper with recommendations to elicit post-traumatic growth. First, you can talk to a therapist to discover and develop coping strategies. Almost everything you read about your mental health will start with self-care, something I believe to be an imperative. In Chapter 9 you'll learn more about SHED, which stands for sleep, hydration, exercise, and diet. Combined, these result in stress reduction.

Finding meaning helps people move forward in their life. You can read books and articles and join support groups. There is little research here because post-traumatic growth is relatively new, but there is increasing evidence that it is a real phenomenon.

In another article, "A Model to Predict Psychological and Health-Related Adjustments in Men with Prostate Cancer: The Role of Post Traumatic Growth, Physical Post Traumatic Growth, Resilience and Mindfulness," Walsh and colleagues explored how PTG is connected to mindfulness, resilience, depression, anxiety, and quality of life. They also explore the idea of physical post-traumatic growth, which supports PTG in cancer survivors.[13]

One key factor in PTG is learning to let go of negative thoughts, emotions, fear, resentment, and anger. This is easier said than done, and the work of Walsh and colleagues suggests it is a process. It take time to heal, but we can come out stronger.

Do This Now

- **Search for the positive and look for the silver lining.** There is something positive, but you may have to work to find it, and it may not always be easy. It can take time to process trauma or adversity.
- **Find meaning in trauma by looking at what you learned about yourself and the nature of our world.** While doing this work, recognize what you will do differently in the future. This is the value of adversity.
- **Be grateful for what you still have, especially if you have post-traumatic growth.**

7

How to Live Happily with Political Divisiveness

HERE IN THE United States, we are experiencing extreme political divisiveness. We are sharply divided by our differing opinions, ideologies, beliefs, and political values. Over time, our news channels, our social media, and our politicians have led us to a place where we are now two warring factions destabilizing our society. Both sides accuse the other of destroying our country and risking our democracy, when the real danger *is* political divisiveness.

As I have already confessed, I am post-political. Current US political discourse is coarse and wholly unproductive, with many politicians telling voters they need "someone who will fight for you." Great! So our leaders argue, demean each other, make false accusations, and obstruct any initiative that belongs to the "other side." The only consensus in our politics is that Democrats and Republicans hate each other.

You can and should vote for the people who represent your politics and values, but you will be more negative if you make politics your identity or, worse, your religion. First, you are more than your politics. When you allow yourself to be consumed by political arguments, fear-mongering, and the talking points of the day, less of you is left for things that are, arguably, more important. Channel your energy into what you value most and what brings you joy. (To clarify, feeling schadenfreude when your side wins a petty argument or election doesn't count as joy.) Second, a focus on politics will all but ensure you are more negative than positive.

Politics in the United States has been a rowdy affair since we decided to overthrow the largest superpower on earth, England, which is today our closest ally. Even the Revolutionary War split the population of the colonies into thirds, with one group supporting revolution, one opposing the uprising, and a third taking a neutral stance. You might also remember that less than 100 years later, we had a Civil War, which is still responsible for the greatest loss of American soldiers.

What has held us together since 1776 are our values and our shared belief that the United States is special because it is built on compromise. I believe it is special and worth defending. I hope you feel this way too.

A Short History of How We Got Here

In 1978, CNN started airing a political show called *Crossfire* where a liberal pundit, Tom Braden, and a conservative pundit, Pat Buchanan, faced off. While they argued over current events, they were polite, and it was clear they liked each other. Ted Turner, the founder and owner of CNN, gave the two political commentators the 11:30 p.m. time slot because he wasn't convinced anyone would watch. *Crossfire* turned out to be a success, and CNN soon moved it to a popular 7:30 p.m. time slot. It aired until 2005, when CNN decided to trade political clashes for more moderate, in-depth news coverage.

In 2006, Roger Ailes, the CEO of Rupert Murdoch's Fox News, supposedly said, "We're in the business of feeding people red meat. We're not in the business of giving them broccoli." In that same year, MSNBC launched, feeding red meat to the other half of the political spectrum. There was likely a political motivation for starting these cable television shows, but these channels were part of a business strategy to build a large, stable audience by speaking to their political fears. These channels encouraged people to see things as binary: us versus them, good versus evil, right versus wrong. Now we have two factions who have been shaped by a diet of messages designed to confirm their beliefs and stoke their fears. Politicians and their advisors use these factions to secure votes and to jam a political wedge between voters and the candidate they might have supported. We have been manipulated this way for a long enough time that we finally find ourselves here.

Back in the 1990s, there wasn't a great way to fight with people about politics, outside of Thanksgiving dinner with your Uncle Enrico (the conspiracy theorist). But by the early 2000s, Facebook and Twitter had made it convenient for people to pick fights with friends, relatives, acquaintances, public figures, and strangers.

Many people have argued about politics on Facebook and Twitter, even unfriending their parents and lifelong friends. You likely know people who won't watch a television show if a lead actor has the wrong politics. And some celebrities suggest that they don't want you watching their show if you have different political opinions.

Removing the Sources of Negativity

People who are overly political are miserable when their preferred candidate loses to a political rival. That happens about half the time. Why be upset, angry, negative, and anxious every four years? Vote on Election Day, then focus on your daily life.

I haven't watched network news in longer than I can remember. I removed it from my media diet, listening instead to CNBC as my source of news, because the politicians who speak with Andrew Ross-Sorkin, Becky Quick, and Joe Kernan tend to be on their best behavior because the moneyed class is listening. I subscribe to the *New York Times* (meaning I must be a liberal) and the *Wall Street Journal* (which must mean I am a conservative). The truth is that I am an omnivore who assesses the state of our society and loves reading good writers. I am impervious to politics, and I hope your candidate wins their election the next time you vote. But right now, we need to spend some time learning how people become infected with politics in the first place. Let us now enter the meme machine.

Memetic Infections

My friend Howard Bloom wrote a book titled *The Lucifer Principle: A Scientific Expedition into the Forces of History.* You don't know Howard, but you do know his work before he started writing science books. He was the publicist for Aerosmith, Joan Jett, John Mellencamp, ZZ Top, and AC/DC. He is also the person who forced ABC to sign Prince. While they didn't like Prince, I am positive they were quite happy with *Purple Rain* and the millions of green slips of paper finding their way into their bank accounts.

The Lucifer Principle is a book about memes, but not the cute videos of cats or babies. The word *meme* is shortened version of the word *memetics*, which is the study of human cultures, our social systems, and how we come to believe things. When the evolutionary biologist Richard Dawkins coined the term *meme* in a book titled *The Selfish Gene*, he was comparing the gene's ability to replicate, mutate, and spread to ideas, which seem to do the same thing.

It is likely you believe you have ideas. But the truth is that ideas have you. Your faith tradition is probably the same as your parents. Your beliefs, customs, cultures, and language were all installed in you through the various memes that possess you. You don't really believe you left the womb with a deep devotion to a progressive or conservative cause, do you?

When something goes viral, there are several factors at work. Memes are generally easy to understand and communicate to others, making it easy to pass on. They also cause strong emotions, making them memorable. Memes are relatable and make it easy to identify with them. They are versatile and show up in different contexts, allowing them to infect communities. Repetition causes memes to gain traction. When someone repeats a meme like "Make America Great Again" or "Build Back Better," they cause it to spread.

Once you know ideas have you, you are free to uninstall them. You can wind down your heavy diet of politics and decide to stop looking at the world through a narrow, distorted lens that generates a negative view of your world and your friends and family.

Why No One Wants to Sit Next to Uncle Enrico

There is something alluring about conspiracy theories. They provide the person listening an explanation of events they don't understand. These conspiracies are memes, and many of them tend to spread. They speak to the person who believes rich and powerful people are pulling the strings (something that has always been true—just saying). This also provides proof of nefarious actors impacting the listener's life. I believe everyone has the right to exactly one conspiracy, preferably Bigfoot, a faked moon landing, or the assassination of JFK— you know, the safe ones. Let's call this the third narrative, the concept of a conspiracy narrative.

Thanks to the internet, social media, and the algorithms that infect minds with the idea that everything is a conspiracy, there are more people who now hold this view. If you know a lot of conspiracy-oriented people you will know they are fearful, sometimes paranoid, and more negative about their life, even if they have never been personally harmed by any of the conspiracies. On Thanksgiving, your Uncle Enrico or Aunt Jenny can't stop trying to spread the meme, infecting others with the conspiracy. Meanwhile, others escape to the children's table to avoid talking about political conspiracies. Uncle Enrico, Aunt Jenny, and others infected with the meme lose their ability to talk about anything else but conspiracies.

Conspiracy theories are complex. From a psychological point of view, one way you are infected by conspiracy is through your cognitive biases. There is a pattern recognition called apophenia, which allows the person to see connections where none exist. Sociologists look at how conspiracy theories spread in social groups. These theories are a tool for social cohesion in groups.

One of our problems with politics is that both sides use conspiracy theories to discredit their opponents, spread misinformation, and use them to assassinate a person's character. Our social media platforms have made it easier to spread conspiracies farther and faster.

I am certain that any population of 335 million people is certain to find some part engaged in a conspiracy. Outside of the occasional email invitation to join the Illuminati, I have yet to be invited to participate in a conspiracy, but I have noticed that cable television channels invite their viewers to become entrenched in partisan politics and conspiracies.

Let me invite you to join me in the conspiracy of positivity in a world full of negative politics.

Our Life with Two Warring Narratives

Our society is dominated by two narratives. One narrative is designed to speak to one segment of our population. The second narrative is built for the other half of the population. Every day, the news channels feed you with talking points, removing any context that might create a more realistic take on the day's crisis. The last time we shared a common narrative was 9/11, and even that was short lived as the politics over new entities like the Patriot Act and the Department of Homeland Security caused a political rift.

The problem with these two narratives is that they are incomplete. A half-truth isn't a truth.

Eric Hoffer was a social philosopher who was awarded the Presidential Medal of Freedom. He wrote 10 books, but his best-known book was his first one, *The True Believer: Thoughts on the Nature of Mass Movements.* Hoffer argued that fanatical and extremist cultural movements arise when many frustrated people, believing their lives to be worthless or spoiled, join a movement demanding radical change. But the real attraction for this population is an escape from the self, not a realization of hopes: "A mass movement attracts and holds a following not because it can satisfy the desire for self-advancement, but because it can satisfy the passion for self-renunciation."[1] Hoffer also offered up this insight: "The desire to belong is partly a desire to lose oneself."[2]

"And it is the certitude of his infallible doctrine that renders the true believer impervious to the uncertainties, surprises and the unpleasant realities of the world around him."[3] When you are infected with politics, it can cause you to be unable to see or accept another person's perspective.

Liminal Thinking

Dave Gray is a visual thinking expert and an author of several books, including *Liminal Thinking: Create the Change You Want By Changing the Way You Think*. Liminal means occupying both sides of a boundary. Gray suggests that our beliefs make up our models of reality and that we created our own convictions. Our beliefs create our world, and at the same time they create blind spots.

Gray argues our beliefs shape our reality, and that by understanding and changing our beliefs, we can create change in our lives and in the world around us. He provides a few tools and techniques for accomplishing this, including suspending our judgment, emptying your cup (letting go of our beliefs), cross-checking, asking questions, and establishing contacts. Here are a few takeaways from Gray's book:

- If you want to loosen politics' grip on you, consider Gray's recommendation that you suspend judgment to make it easier to avoid conflict. By practicing suspending your judgment, you can allow your political friend to talk without arguing. I have suspended my judgment for many years.
- Gray's second strategy is to cross-check claims. It isn't difficult to confirm claims on the internet even though you may have to sort through an abundance of disinformation, misinformation, and straight-out political lies. If you can find a reliable source, you may find out that your political opponent was right about the data.
- Gray's third strategy is to ask questions. If confronted by a political type, ask them some questions. First, you must be aware if the person expressing their opinion did no real research beyond watching Tucker Carlson or Rachel

Maddow to pick up the talking points. Second, they will say they researched their claim, which often means watching YouTube. YouTube is designed to feed people content that reinforces their most extreme beliefs, and its algorithm pushes people to the furthest wing of the political spectrum.[4]

Our political system is split into two sets of beliefs. This tension between political parties is a feature, not a bug. The left and the right check each other, preventing either side from going too far too fast. The governance process allows our country to move forward at a moderate pace. We need both narratives because we have two wings. The nature of those two wings is what allows for democracy to flourish because our system is designed to work when both parties compromise. A problem occurs when each side insists that the existence of the other puts our democracy in danger. The real threat is the negative, immature, and increasingly hostile attitudes of both of our political parties, who are supposed to find consensus, but behave like children instead.

What we should want from our politicians would sound like this: "My dear friend and colleague has great intentions, and she is right about this issue. We are great friends and very much enjoy working together. Where we disagree is on the financial resources and how to pay for her important program. We are committed to working on this together to find a way to do what we can to make things better." If our politicians were brave enough to agree that there is something valid in what the other party wants, we might find that there is a way to do something, even if one side wishes it were more while the other side wishes it were a little less.

How to Live with Other People's Politics

I am certain you can live with other people's politics. In fact, you have been doing so your entire life. Approximately half of the country has politics opposite yours. Yet, you are still here, and to me, you seem to be unharmed by President Trump or President Biden. You have family and friends infected by the opposite meme to the one you are carrying and potentially spreading. You have neighbors who have the wrong political sign in their front yard during election years, yet they are still your friends.

Like your faith tradition, you are allowed your politics, and others are allowed theirs. Unless you would try converting your friends and neighbors to change their religion from Lutheranism to the Church of Satan, there is no reason to try arguing them into adopting your political position.

If you are brave enough to become post-political, I can assure you it will reduce your negativity. Spend one weekend reading each candidate's positions, vote in November, and then leave it for two years, in which time you will enjoy feeling better.

Preventing Political Negativity

Let's start working on removing the memes that cause political divisiveness. This is difficult if your politics is your identity. But having removed my political memes, I know it is possible. Consider whether you want to be more positive more of the time. Now ask yourself if you're willing to trade your memes for increased positivity. Think about whether you believe that you have friends, family, neighbors, and colleagues who are your enemies because they are infected with the other meme.

If you think you would rather not believe that, you should immediately start to uninstall your dogmatic political belief.

As we start dealing with this potent source of negativity, you might look around and notice that hyper-partisan people are also more negative than those who aren't consumed by politics. Think back to your first day of a notoriously difficult college class. Imagine the professor said, "Look to the left of you and the right. One of you will be gone by the end of the semester." Now, look at the people you interact with on a daily basis. If you don't see anyone more political than you, it might be time for you to change.

If you're not convinced, here is some research to back me up. A longitudinal study analyzed sentiment and emotion in news headlines between 2000 and 2019. It applied Ekman's six basic emotions (anger, disgust, fear, joy, sadness, surprise) and a neutral label to categorize the headlines. The results reveal that headlines across all news media became more negative over that time period.[5] As the researchers state, "The chronological analysis of headlines emotionality shows a growing proportion of headlines denoting *anger*, *fear*, *disgust* and *sadness* and a decrease in the prevalence of emotionally *neutral* headlines across the studied outlets over the 2000–2019 interval."[6] Consuming media that feeds you fear is the equivalent of consuming poison every day.

Another paper, "Politics is making us sick: The Negative Impact of Political Engagement on Public Health During the Trump Administration," analyzed how key physical, mental, and social health indicators changed during the Trump administration.[7] The study wasn't about President Trump, but rather our health during a time of extreme political tension.

The author notes that the mechanism by which politics can harm health is relatively well understood. Politics is a chronic stressor, saturating popular culture and permeating daily life through social media, various entertainment platforms, and a 24-hour news cycle.[8] The negative effects of politics on social well-being—whether through passive attention or active engagement—are documented by several existing studies.

Based on a 32-item survey specifically designed to measure the health-related impacts of political engagement, Smith estimated that 94 million Americans perceived politics as a significant source of stress, 44 million had lost sleep because of politics, nearly 30 million reported politics had harmed their physical health, and 11 million had suicidal thoughts because of politics. The full 32-item battery has four subscales: physical health, emotional health, regretted behavior (e.g., "I have vowed to spend less time on politics but failed to follow through"), and social and lifestyle health.[9]

Smith's research reminds me of a quote by Henry Adams, the grandson of President John Quincy Adams and the great-grandson of John Adams: "Politics, as a practice, whatever its professions, has always been the systematic organization of hatreds."

In 2018, Alan I. Abramowitz and Steven W. Webster researched the phenomenon of Americans aligning *against* one political party rather than supporting the other. This trend has likely increased in recent years, and it shapes our society in various ways. For example, Americans have extremely negative views of both political parties. In 2016, Democrats scored Republicans a 23 on a scale from 0 to 100. The Republicans, for their part, gave Democrats a generous 27 on that same scale. Independents have an even more negative view of both parties, with a 46 for Democrats and 44 for Republicans.[10] (If you think that's extreme, you should have seen the studies on wearing masks during the COVID-19 pandemic. Wow!)

According to Abramowitz and Webster, a combination of cultural issues, partisan media, and polarization creates our divisiveness.[11] This has a negative effect on individuals and US society. On the individual level, people who have a political affiliation consistently engage in confirmation bias that confirms their existing beliefs. Abramowitz and Webster's research echoes that of Hoffer in that they agree that political affiliation predicts how vulnerable a person is to disinformation. Confirmation bias makes partisans far more likely to believe disinformation, even when it is presented as obviously false.[12] This can also encourage people to see those with different viewpoints as a threat, which weakens social bonds and feeds polarization.

Do This Now

You can combat disinformation by taking the following steps.

- **Identify sensational headlines.** When you see something that seems misleading or jarring, don't take it at face value.
- **Verify the source.** Can you tell where the information originated? Look for an affiliation from the author and anyone quoted in the article. Consider whether the publication or media outlet is trustworthy, or if they have an overt political agenda.

(Continued)

(Continued)

- **Seek balance.** If you sense bias, look for a story about the same event in a media outlet that tends to have the opposite view. Compare the coverage and try to determine where the truth is. (Hint: It's probably somewhere in the middle.)
- **Maintain skepticism.** If you found an article on social media, be skeptical and look for a more reliable source. If a story appears on only one outlet, be even more skeptical.
- **Don't trust your own biases.** A good way to detect confirmation bias is to consider how you would react if the opposite party had done the exact same thing. If you agree with an action, it shouldn't matter who takes it. Don't support something that you wouldn't support if the other side did it.

Before becoming post-political, I was a great at arguing politics, mostly because I read everything, left and right. However, arguing generates negativity (even if you win), so turn off all political media. I know it's difficult, but this is the Negativity Fast and that means you remove all sources of negativity.

If a political foe tries to invite you into an argument, bow out by saying, "You win, I gave up politics." The truth is that avoiding an argument, even one you would enjoy, makes you the winner. If you get the sense that someone is just stepping onto their soapbox, try saying, "You are up on these issues. I'll look into these things soon. Thanks for sharing that with me." Walk away and decide how you'll spend your time and energy so you can make an impact on something worthwhile. (Trying to change someone's mind about politics is a waste of your talents.)

Recognize that you don't want too strong a left, like North Korea, and you don't want too strong a right, like Brazil. You want both sides to be strong enough to act as a check on each other.

It is my great hope that reading this book will help you be more positive more of the time. Later in this book, you are going to start your Negativity Fast, and that means removing all the sources of negativity, including politics, be it Fox News or MSNBC. At this point in our journey to positivity, there is no harm in letting go of your politics. If politics is your identity, you will need a new identity, a positive identity. Let me offer you a new identity as a post-political, positive, happy person who cares enough to vote, without allowing politics to consume you.

8

Wanting and the Perils
of Social Media

THE JONESES SEEM to have the perfect life. Mr. and Mrs. Jones are dazzlingly rich and attractive people. Their two perfect children—one boy and one girl, of course—could be models. They live in an exceptionally beautiful house that looks like a team of realtors staged every square foot. Scrolling through their Instagram, you find pictures of their exotic vacations and unflinchingly joyous expressions. Even at work, Mr. Jones effortlessly collects accolades and achievements, even though you're convinced you put in at least as many hours as he does.

What you don't know about the Joneses is that they are miserable. The things we own eventually own us, including the facade of the perfect life. It isn't easy to pretend that you have the perfect life: It takes time, effort, and money to manufacture every moment.

One downside of social media is that it can cause you to compare yourself with others. Jealousy will make you want what the Joneses have; envy might even make you wish something horrible happens to them. It's easy to make those comparisons without wondering why Mrs. Jones—or Ms. Kardashian—needs you to believe they have the perfect life. Who are they trying to catch up with, and who are they trying to impress? The perfect life is a lie, especially if keeping the public attention requires shocking them into looking.

One reason that you only want what other people have is mimetics, which is not actually the study of escaping from invisible boxes. In a book titled *Wanting: The Power of Mimetic Desire in Everyday Life*, Luke Burgis uses the insights of the French polymath René Girard to explain why we want what we want.[1] Girard was once asked to teach a literature class at Stanford. As he read through the books on the syllabus, he discovered that many of the characters were taught what they should want by other characters, who functioned as models. Girard termed this phenomenon *mimetics*. Not only does mimetics cause you to want something but it also creates rivalry, breeding the envy that makes you want to see people fail. Envy is a powerful and potent type of negativity.[2]

Commenting on this process, Burgis writes, "We live in a time of hyper-imitation. Fascination with what is trending and going viral is symptomatic of our predicament. So is political polarization. It stems in part from mimetic behavior that destroys nuance and poisons even our most honorable goals." But here's the point: We don't start out desiring some object or outcome, then develop jealousy or envy when we can't get it.[3] Instead, we look to a model to discover what we should want in the first place. As Burgis puts it, "Desire requires models—people who endow things with value for us merely because they want these things."

One of my primary professional pursuits is discovering higher-resolution lenses through which to see the world around me and my clients. Burgis offers a very practical and tactical way to do this: "establish and communicate a clear hierarchy of values," which he says offers an "antidote to mimetic conformity." You can do this by naming your values and ranking them. Here is a sample list that may help you escape mimetic desire:

- Health: My health, including my mental health as it allows for my other values.
- Relationships: My family and friends, as well as other relationships.

- Contribution: I want to contribute something positive and valuable for others, including (I hope) this book.
- Wealth: My three Gen Z children are going to have a tough economic experience. I want to be able to help them with their financial challenges.

Remember, the Joneses are human: Even on Instagram, they are dealing with their own struggles and insecurities. So rather than treating evidence of success as evidence of satisfaction, work on surer paths. Spend time with the people you love, pursue your passions, engage in physical activity, and, like you are doing now, keep working on personal development. Real happiness doesn't come from external validation. Half the time, the person validating you is only doing so because it validates them.

If you want to be more positive, ignore the influencers, who are only modeling models who themselves model models (it's models all the way down). It's not automatically bad to want something you don't have, but each of us has different positives and negatives. If you want to be miserable, keep comparing your weaknesses to someone else's positives—especially if they spend most of their energy hiding their negatives.

The Cyber Bullies

When I was in high school, it wasn't unusual for two boys to get into a scuffle over a real or perceived slight. After the scuffle, the conflict was generally over. Not so for girls, who seem less prone to physical violence and more adept at psychological violence. *Mean Girls* might as well be a documentary: A group of popular girls spend the entire movie befriending and then ostracizing a new girl, ultimately treating her with the same cruelty that they use on everyone.

This form of psychological torture has been weaponized through Instagram, Snapchat, TikTok, and Twitter, creating emotional distress for the poor kid who is being bullied. In fact, many young girls have two Instagram accounts: one public and one called a Finsta account, a "Fake Insta" account for their closest friends. Among other things, Finsta accounts allow teenagers to bully one another where their parents can't observe their bad behavior. The consequences can be severe.[4]

- **Emotional and Psychological Problems:** Bullying can cause the person being bullied to experience severe emotional distress. Being harassed or humiliated, whether in public or in private, causes anxiety and low self-esteem. It can also cause them stress and difficulty concentrating.[5]
- **Isolation:** Bullying and cyberbullying are often designed to isolate the person. They may leave social media or isolate themselves from their family and friends. Many students don't yet recognize that the hierarchy of high school (or even grade school and middle school) isn't the hierarchy of real life as an adult.[6]
- **Body Shaming:** Social media can propagate unrealistic body standards and body image perceptions, often through body shaming.[7]
- **Reputation Damage:** It is easy to share false rumors or embarrassing information. Some manipulate images or videos to humiliate their targets, generally to cause social exclusion. My youngest daughter—a strong, beautiful, and charming young woman—once spotted an ex-boyfriend

on her Instagram follower list. His ex-girlfriend posted his photo with this commentary: "looking at one of my followers thinking it would suck to be the ugly twin."

- **Physical Health Issues:** Stress from being bullied can cause headaches, stomachaches, and sleep disturbance. There are long-term impacts from being bullied, including psychological scars and in some cases ongoing mental health problems.[8]

Social media can be a dark and dangerous place, especially for young people. The teenage years may seem difficult without living on Instagram, but the potential for limitless and increasingly vicious bullying is far worse. Parents would do well to look for signs that something is wrong and intervene as early as possible.

Social Media and the Spread of Negativity

Social media is pervasive, which means it is something unwelcome that spreads widely. In fact, spreading negativity is what social media does best. Its algorithms are programmed to give more visibility to content that generates the highest amount of interaction. More often than not, this is extreme political or conspiracy-minded information that people either doggedly believe or despise. This is the natural result of decades of fearmongering by both the legacy media and cable news, but it's presented in a whole new context. Instead of yelling at their TV screens, people can now engage in all-caps tirades, denigrating strangers and "friends" alike.[9] Let's break down how that negativity spreads.

The first way social media spreads negativity is by perpetuating misinformation and fake news. For whatever reason, people are more likely to spread half-truths or even blatantly false information. This content can create fear, confusion, and hostility, especially over politics. And once it's posted, it's easy to share across platforms.[10]

The second way social media spreads negativity is trolling. A troll is a person who provokes others by posting something provocative or irrelevant, with the goal of disrupting the conversation, eliciting an emotional response, or simply sowing discord.[11] The reason most social media platforms allow users to block others is because trolling is so pervasive.

The third way social media passes negativity to others is hate speech and discrimination. I believe the First Amendment headlines the Bill of Rights because it is necessary to avoid tyranny. So far, so good, but freedom of speech often includes the freedom to spread hate. It is, at least relatively, easy to avoid most people who traffic in hatred (even offline). But unfortunately, you can count on there being someone willing to use any event or characteristic in a negative way.[12] Perhaps we should worry less about testing IQ and more about developing character.

The fourth way some use social media to spread negativity far and wide is by creating an echo chamber, polarizing people across entire platforms. Every social media algorithm is designed to show you more of what you have already seen.[13] That's what keeps you on the platform for as long as possible. So do your part: Run more searches for "happy kittens" or "babies laughing" and fewer for "the earth is flat."

Finally, social media uses negativity bias to spread negativity—as we've already seen, people pay more attention to negative news and events, creating a cycle of fear and anxiety.[14] That includes FOMO, fear of missing out. You would do better to have a healthy fear of FOMO.

More Positive Communication

You and I can make a difference, even a small one, by using positive communication on these platforms. Most news follows the principle that if it bleeds, it leads. But it's not just about broadcasting "good news" stories to our networks. When you are on social media, use positive communication and share something helpful. That encourages open-mindedness and well-being, even among people who may disagree with you.

One of Jordan Peterson's rules in *12 Rules for Life* is "Treat Yourself Like Someone You Are Responsible for Helping."[15] Regardless of how you feel about Jordan Peterson, this is solid advice. You can start by speaking to yourself constructively. You may know people who say horrible things about themselves, causing them to be negative. I have heard people I know say, "I am stupid," after making a mistake, or "I never get things right." That kind of generalization doesn't help, no matter how many mistakes you've made. A more positive and helpful communication would be something like, "I made a mistake, and now I can do better next time."

On or off social media, respect other people's opinions and their feelings. They have a different experience not available to you, especially in 140 characters or less. You can start dealing with any disagreements by being open to their perspective and their viewpoint. Learning about other people's paths can help you better understand their perspective. You are under no obligation to agree with a person before you can communicate positively. Research shows that reading fiction can increase your empathy and understanding of others, so why wouldn't listening to another person's story do the same? I have written a blog post every day since December 28, 2009, except for the 13 days I spent in Tibet (despite the fact that Basecamp 1 on Mount Everest had better Wi-Fi than my home in Columbus, Ohio). Many of those posts arise from other people's stories.

Sometimes, positive communication means keeping your (virtual) mouth shut. One time, while I was sitting on an airplane waiting for takeoff, I got a call from a friend of mine. He breathlessly told me that a random guy in England—a full-grown adult man—was tweeting something negative about me to my followers on Twitter. My friend suggested we take him down. I asked him to spread the word: Do not engage. My friend thought I was being magnanimous, but the truth is that I would only empower this person by responding to his attack. Sure enough, this poor fellow spent two or three days trolling without result, then he gave up. I have always lived by the idea that "you should never worry about the opinions of people who are not going to attend your funeral." That means about eight billion people or so aren't worth stressing about.

More Contacts, Less Connection

Robin Dunbar is a sociologist in England who spent several years studying chimpanzees. You really don't want to be a chimp. You'd spend your days walking around to find food, mostly leaves that require a lot of time and energy to eat and digest. Between the long walks, the eating, and picking nits out of other chimps' fur, there isn't much time left for other endeavors. A tribe of chimps is limited to a small number because they can only manage so many relationships.

Dunbar has applied his findings about network size to humans, even those of us who aren't quite so furry. The average human, he found, can manage around 150 relationships, even though some are able to go up to 225.[16] I have 85,000 followers on Twitter and 54,000 followers on LinkedIn, mostly because I create content in areas where people need help: sales, leadership, and doing good work. These numbers are so much larger than Dunbar's number that it feels like folly to form relationships with my followers. I know a lot of people without knowing a lot of people.

Like you, I have more contacts and less connection. Your contacts may deserve some small sliver of your time and energy, especially in professional settings. But devote most of it to your 150 (or so) relationships, your real connections.

We Sold Our Attention

Of all the damage social media causes, there may be nothing worse than consenting to give up our precious attention. When Apple released the screen time feature, people were stunned at how many hours they expended staring into a screen. According to Techjury.net, teenagers between ages 13 and 17 spend an average of 8 hours and 39 minutes a day with their screens, largely on social media. Adults between 18 and 29 spend 5 hours or more each day, with a gradual decline in the 30–49 group (4–5 hours a day) and the over 50 group (less than 4 hours a day).[17] In terms of gender, males spend almost 11 hours a day on social media, while females spend more than 12 hours. And in a single year, an average male logs 4,015 hours on social media, while an average female racks up 4,365 hours. By comparison, an average work year is 2,080 hours, just half the time we spend on social media, and we still take up many of our work hours with more social media. My thumb hurts just thinking about all that scrolling.

The reason you don't pay for social media, blue check-marks aside, is because the platforms sell your attention to advertisers. The algorithms are designed to show you what you want, and ultimately to tell you what you should want. Every time you doom scroll, you're both a buyer and a product.

The High Cost of Social Media Usage

You may have noticed that you have more connections with people you have never met but fewer relationships. That comes with more transactional communications and fewer conversations. We spend more time with screens and social media apps than we spend with people, and even real-life gatherings often find people tethered to their phones. Now people even want to work from home, safe and secure in their solitary technological pods, typing notes to other pod dwellers.

We are not meant to be alone. We are meant to be with people, and we need to stop paying for social media with our relationships. Why do we feel the need to distract ourselves with tiny jolts of virtual dopamine? What are we running from?

My office features a painting of the socialist, atheist, and polemicist Christopher Hitchens, one of my favorite writers. I commissioned an artist to paint Hitchens, to remind me that as a writer, I should never be guilty of being boring. After being diagnosed with esophageal cancer, Hitchens wrote in *Vanity Fair* that "you must choose your future regrets," a powerful idea from a man who knew all too well that he was running out of time.

Choosing in Real Life

We are 15 minutes from the Matrix, but one where people willingly escape into a metaverse so they can hide from reality. Yuval Noah Harari, the author of *Sapiens*, suggests the future will be one where people will be drugged and connected to the metaverse or video games, a vision so dystopian that it could only come from an intellectual.[18] Whatever content social media delivers, it isn't better than real life. One way to remove negativity is to spend time with people in real life, preferably without a screen in sight. Start with your family and your friends, because it will boost your positivity to spend time with people you love.

How to Live Without Negative Social Media

You may want to use your Negativity Fast to undergo a digital detox, where you swear off social media for some period. You might sleep better, for instance, if you stop scrolling well before bedtime. It is likely that you have ingested all kinds of nasty negative content, so fasting from it for a week or two is a good first step.

If you're genuinely addicted to social media, though, you're going to need another strategy. One mistake I made when I did my first 30-day Negativity Fast was removing negativity without adding anything positive. Even social media can be positive, if you use it for education, positive social change, or genuine connections with people you love. So I altered my plan: Rather than giving up social media altogether, I spent the next 60 days ingesting only positive media content. If you are going to keep social media, follow accounts that promote positivity or ones that teach new skills.

We are inching closer to starting your Negativity Fast, which means soon you will have to begin removing your sources of negativity. You can prepare by deciding which content you will ingest during your fast. Fair warning: I will eventually try to convince you to avoid adding negativity back into your diet later, but one step at a time.

Do This Now

Replace sources of negativity with accounts that promote positivity. Instead of scrolling through the stream, waiting for something to grab your attention, proactively build a list of people who are positive, optimistic, future-oriented, and empowered.

1. Examine your Twitter, Instagram, Facebook, and YouTube feeds one by one. Remove any accounts that don't support your new approach. That includes anything negative, overtly political, or designed to make you angry or fearful. If you don't feel comfortable unfriending or unfollowing someone you know who posts negative content, block them instead.
2. Keep all the positive people and positive content.
3. Add new accounts that will support your positive social media intake. Here is a list of positive people you can follow: @powerofpositivity (Instagram only), Tim Ferris, Lewis Howes, Mel Robbins, Brené Brown, Oprah, Reese Witherspoon, Cal Newport (YouTube only), Jocko Willink, Robin Sharma, Bob Burg, Hector LaMarque, Ryan Holiday, and Jay Shetty.

4. Stay vigilant and don't get sucked into ads that are designed to spark negative feelings. As you consume more positive content and less negative content, the sponsored posts in your feed should reflect that change.

5. Consider removing TikTok completely from your and your children's devices. Recently, CNN reported that "the non-profit Center for Countering Digital Hate (CCDH) found that it can take less than three minutes after signing up for a TikTok account to see content related to suicide and about five more minutes to find a community promoting eating disorder content."[19] No new dance move is worth that risk.

The Science of Social Media and Negativity

In a paper titled "Social Media Use and Adolescents' Well-Being: Developing a Typology of Person-Specific Effect Patterns," it was found that a passive use of social media where one is not actively engaged "has been shown to have a negative impact on well-being" in part because of the upward comparison to others.[20] We are back to the Joneses and avoiding trying to keep up.

Another a paper, called "Increases in Serious Psychological Distress among Ontario Students between 2013 and 2017: Assessing the Impact of Time Spent on Social Media," found that increased time on social media can cause "higher levels of psychological distress among adolescents."[21] Those of us who grew up without social media may underestimate how harmful social media can be. But if you can remember how difficult your early teenage years were, it might cause you to try to help them cope. You and I know that the king and queen of the prom are no longer a big deal.

"Left- and Right-Leaning News Organizations' Negative Tweets Are More Likely to be Shared," according to another article. The last thing that we need is greater political divisiveness.[22] You see a lot of these tweets in your feed. It can be challenging to let them go by without comment, but you are not going to change anyone's opinion, and no one will change yours. Block them!

"Social Media and Well-Being: Pitfalls, Progress, and Next Steps" suggests, "Overall, the impact of social media on well-being is multifaceted and depends on various factors such as usage patterns, content exposure and individual characteristics. Further research is needed to better understand these complexities and develop a more nuanced understanding of the relationship between social media and well-being."[23] I believe we now know that the algorithm can be dangerous and cause harm to our well-being.

As a content creator with over 5,000 blog posts and a presence on Twitter, LinkedIn, and YouTube, I stay away from posting things that are negative. I also consume very little from these platforms. When I do, I consume what is positive and recommend that you do the same.

- If you are going to use the social platforms, try to limit the time you spend on social media and limit the people you follow to those who are positive.
- Stay away from provocative content and people who are negative. Block anyone who is trying to stir up controversy or itching for an argument.
- When you post on a social media, make sure your content it positive and helpful.

- Block anyone who is overtly negative. Make a list of people who are happy, healthy, and positive.
- Don't compare yourself with others. You see only what looks good without knowing what's behind the facade.

This is the Negativity Fast, so you want to remove negativity in all its sources.

9

How to Change Your State

WHEN MY CHILDREN were young, they would occasionally have a meltdown. If you have children, you know they can manifest a negative state in themselves and you in a matter of seconds. Rather than giving into the three little terrorists' demands, my strategy was to run away from them—fast. It was difficult for their little diaper-bound legs to keep pace, especially when I ran upstairs. The reason I was running is because it broke their state, causing them to start laughing. It felt like a game. It didn't take long for them to remember they were supposed to be upset, at which point it was time to run again. Why should I allow these tiny humans to change my state? Instead, I would change their state.

As they grew older and complained about what they were not allowed to do, I would sing Veruca Salt's song "I Want It Now" from *Willie Wonka & the Chocolate Factory* that starts with the line, "I want the world. I want the whole world. I want to lock it all up in my pocket." The other two children and Cher would join in until our little Veruca gave up and went to their room, leaving us in sweet silence. These strategies were my way of changing their state. (If you have small children, you can thank me for these strategies.)

When one of our kids needed to be punished, I would make them sit in my office so we could "talk about character." I can speak for close to three hours on a single breath. After an hour or so listening to me talk, a teenage child would try to give me the key to their car and ask me to ground them. Instead, I would keep them long enough that they would not repeat their high crime or misdemeanor. One of my twin daughters started to bring her friends to my office when they needed someone to talk to. The goal was always to change their mental state.

Changing your mental state will work equally well for you. There are several things you can do to change your negative state to neutral or even positive. Choose a few of the following strategies that you believe will help you most.

Running Away from Negativity

It is close to impossible to maintain a negative state when you are running. You might be angry and ticked off about something for the first few minutes. But as soon as you start breathing heavy and sweating, your negative state will subside.[1] Have you ever noticed that when you are angry, you tend to hold your breath? Your anger keeps your diaphragm high, depriving you of oxygen. As soon as you start breathing again, your negativity will start to wane. Shallow, upper chest breathing is part of typical stress response. Abdominal breathing helps to control the nervous system and encourages the body to relax, bringing about a range of health benefits.[2]

If running isn't your thing, try picking up heavy weights to get the same outcome. Your emotional state and your physiological state are closely linked. When you change one, you also change the other. Any physical activity can release endorphins, chemicals in the brain that lift your mood. Physical activity is also an excellent distraction that can help you break out of a negative mindset.

Nutrition and Hydration

Low blood sugar, high blood sugar, or a poor diet can make you feel physically and emotionally unwell. For example, a sugary, fatty meal might help you feel good for a short time, but soon you'll feel completely drained. Eating something healthy can improve your state, give you long-lasting energy, and provide your brain with the nutrients it needs to function well. No, chocolate isn't healthy, and it may lead you straight to a sugar crash. I recommend lean protein, some leafy greens, and some crunchy fruits, nuts, and vegetables.

Proactively hydrating can prevent you from falling into a negative state in the first place. If you start to feel sluggish and down, try drinking enough water that your bladder files a lawsuit for not being paid for overtime.

Remember to Breathe

There are other ways you can turn your negative emotional state positive. One easy way to address negative emotional states is through mindful breathing. This simple practice starts by inhaling for a count of four, hold it for another count of four, exhaling for a count of four, and waiting for a count of four to inhale.

Talk to Others

Spending time with positive people who support you is an excellent way to change your state. It could be your family, friends, or positive people at work. Talking things out with others can remove your negative state, especially if you avoid venting. Be cautious about who you turn to when you need a boost. While it can be fun to gripe with a fellow complainer, this cannot shift your state from negative to positive. Talk to people who know how to distract you, help you gain some perspective, and move past whatever's bothering you. You can't change your state if you're talking to another miserable person.

Turn to Music

Music can also help you make a change, especially something with energy. For me, it's' AC/DC's "For Those About to Rock We Salute You" or Van Halen's "Unchained." You, however, might choose Taylor Swift's "Shake It Off," and who could blame you? Recent research suggests that listening to high-energy music can increase feelings of excitement and arousal, which may lead to a greater willingness to take action and make changes.[3] Additional studies have demonstrated that music with a fast tempo and strong beat can enhance exercise performance and increase motivation.[4] Therefore, it can be concluded that music with energy has the potential to inspire and empower individuals to make positive changes in their lives.

Your Gratitude Journal

You learned about using a gratitude journal in Chapter 5. Pausing long enough to write about what you can and should be grateful for can help you be more positive. It's a great way to change your state because it encourages you to focus on something you appreciate. The science on gratitude is rich. Even though you might believe that can't be all that effective, the people who study it seem to find it to be powerful when it comes to reducing negativity.

Positive Affirmations

In Chapter 1 we explored how our inner dialogue can cause us to be negative. Positive affirmations can help you override that negative voice and replace it with an encouraging one.

You can talk yourself into a better mood by focusing on the positive and giving yourself the same kind of reassurance you'd offer a friend on a rough day. You should be careful not to say anything negative to or about yourself. Some people will tell you that your brain will believe whatever you continually tell yourself.

Yoga or Tai Chi

If you are reading this book while wearing Lululemon, then this is for you. It can be uplifting to unroll your mat and do a little downward-facing dog. Focusing on physical movements and poses helps you find your breath and calm your nervous system.[5,6]

Nature Therapy

Nature therapy or ecotherapy is simply spending time in nature to help shift your mindset. Spending time in nature can reduce your anger, stress, and fear.[7] You may experience something numinous, which is something awe-inspiring, supernatural, or spiritual. Some of the best thinkers, like Nietzsche, have spent time walking in nature. It was where they would go to think.

Acts of Kindness

To forget yourself and your negativity, focus on others who need help. This is one of the most potent strategies for changing your negative state. You will feel better, and you will feel better about yourself when you help someone. (We'll talk more about this in Chapter 11.)

Avoid Alcohol and Drugs

It is a good idea to avoid alcohol and drugs generally, but if you are in a negative headspace, avoid them at all costs. For many people they trigger anxiety and depression, and they can destabilize your mood.

The Evolution of Laughter

It is true that laughter reduces stress. It can cause you to have a sense of well-being. Perhaps its evolutionary purpose is to help us cope with negative events.[8] In the book *Human Evolution* by Robin Dunbar, the author suggests that "there is one behavior that might allow several people to be 'groomed' simultaneously: laughter." He continues to suggest laughter from grooming at a distance can trigger your endorphins. Dunbar also suggests that laughter spreads easily. I believe that this is one way we cope with stress.[9]

Emotional Freedom Technique

This is something called "tapping." I confess I have never tried this technique, but I know people who use EFT regularly. It's something close to acupuncture, where you tap on certain points on the body, such as your cheekbone and your forehead. I know people who do this, but I was unable to find any science around this practice. In the paper "The Emotional Freedom Technique: Finally, a Unifying Theory for the Practice of Holistic Nursing, or Too Good to True?" the authors write, "More than 60 research articles in peer-reviewed journals report a staggering 98% efficacy rate with the use of this procedure from psychological distress (posttraumatic stress disorder, phobias, anxiety, depression, etc.)."[10]

Pet Therapy

I live with two dogs and two cats. Christopher Hitchens said if you feed, water, and walk a dog, it will believe that you are God, while if you feed, water, and pet a cat, it believes it is God. Whether you're a cat person or a dog person, pets can reduce stress and anxiety and improve your mood. My tiny girl dog, Chelsea, was diagnosed with cancer, so I spent $20,000 dollars for her radiation treatments. When my friend suggested I should have put her down, I explained that I couldn't give up on a fellow sentient being. I was lucky that I could do for Chelsea what I'd do for any family member—and I didn't think twice about it. Chelsea has been with us for six years since her surgeries.

Power Nap

Finally, we have reached my preferred strategy for changing my state. When I am in a particularly foul mood, I lie down on the bed and take a 20-minute nap to reset. Our moods or negative states are innate parts of being human, so all our emotions serve a purpose. Even so, I recommend that you avoid lingering in a negative state, especially if one of these strategies will quickly help you feel more positive.

Let me remind you that you have permission to be negative, even while you are on your Negativity Fast. If you are feeling negative, understand that it's okay to sit with your negativity for a while. That might be exactly what you should do. Don't believe that you need to change states if you don't want to or don't feel ready.

Take Better Care of Yourself

About six weeks before writing this chapter, I quit coffee and sugar at the same time. The first night after giving up coffee, I couldn't sleep. My whole body hurt. I started drinking black coffee when I was thirteen. I knew I liked it as soon as I smelled it—ah coffee! But my heartburn was bothering me, and I do everything in my power to avoid taking pharmaceuticals. I don't drink alcohol, and I don't smoke.

My heart doctor told me the most important thing I needed to do is to lose weight, so sugar was out. In five weeks, I lost 21 pounds. I also started drinking a lot more water. I sleep seven and half hours instead of six.

Your physical health is a ginormous variable when it comes to your mental state. When we don't take care of ourselves, it is easy to go straight negative because we don't feel well. If you want to be more positive more of the time, taking care of yourself will help you get there. What follows here is called SHED (sleep, hydration, exercise, and diet), and it is the foundation of your positivity.

Sleep: The Best Meditation

If you asked me what change you should make first to improve your state, I would suggest sleeping longer. Adding an hour to the time you sleep will help you feel better, making it more likely you can maintain a positive disposition throughout the day. The Dalai Lama will tell you the "best meditation is sleep."[11] This is a twofer. You can sleep more and tell your friends you meditate seven and half hours a day.

Hydration: You Are Mostly Water

The second change you might need to make to stave off negativity is to drink more water. I wonder what people in my office think when I walk to the bathroom every hour. No one says anything, but they must believe I have a tiny bladder. The real reason is that I take hydration seriously. One of the reasons your physiology causes you to feel bad is because you are dehydrated. You know those headaches you get from time to time? That is likely because you were pretending to be a camel.

Exercise: Move Your Body

You will activate all kinds of goodness by exercising regularly because it activates your endorphins, your feel-great neurotransmitters. When endorphins are released in your brain, you have an increased sense of well-being and a reduced sense of pain. You'll have more energy, which will help you maintain your positivity throughout the day. You don't have to do CrossFit, unless you are dead set on having rotator cuff surgery or a brand new knee. An easier way to exercise is to walk.

Diet: Eat Healthy Most of the Time

Tim Ferris would tell you to make Saturday "Faturday." So you eat clean all week, and take Saturday off. Dana White, from the UFC, has a day he calls "F***-It Friday," where he eats something that has no nutritional value or something weird. The less processed foods in your diet, the better. You may need to eat something to maintain your blood sugar to feel good. In this case, some complex carbohydrates like whole-grain cereal, fruit, or vegetables and hummus can help keep you satiated. Other people, like me, feel better by practicing intermittent fasting. On many days, I follow the one-meal-a-day approach because I have greater energy when I don't eat. The most important thing is to listen to your body and provide it with nutritious fuel.

How to Be an Optimist

I was born an optimist. I have always believed things are going to be better in the future, even though the 21st century seems to have other plans for us. You don't have to worry about pessimists, because they already believe things are bad and getting worse. The pessimist says, "It can't get any worse!" And the optimist replies, "Oh, yes it can!"

Martin Seligman is a leading psychologist studying pessimism and optimism. He documented his research in *Learned Optimism: How to Change Your Mind and Your Life*. Here is what Seligman says about pessimists: "The defining characteristic of pessimists is that they tend to believe bad events will last a long time, will undermine everything they do, and are their own fault."[12]

Seligman has this to say about optimists facing the same event: "The optimists . . . tend to believe it is just a temporary setback . . . . Circumstances, bad luck, or other people brought it about. Confronted by a bad situation, they perceive it as a challenge and try harder."

It turns out that, as Seligman says, "pessimism is escapable." Optimists are healthier, live longer, get fewer infectious diseases, and have better health habits and stronger immune systems. When it comes to achievement, success may require more than talent and desire. Seligman suggests optimism may be necessary.[13]

Seligman's research shows that self-talk, our inner voice, is a vital part of optimism. While it's nice to make positive statements to ourselves in good times, they have little effect on our overall positivity. However, what we think when we fail is crucial. The central skill of optimism is tapping into the power of "non-negative thinking." When faced with a setback, optimists are able to encourage themselves to push through a negative experience. Pessimists are unable to change their own destructive self-talk. But there's an upside: With practice, it gets easier to ignore our inner critic and tune into our inner champion.

Do This Now

To build your positive-thinking abilities, follow these four steps.

1. Pay Attention to Your Negative Thoughts

The first step to becoming an optimist is to start paying attention to your negative thoughts. Write them down and see if you can reframe them to make them neutral, or at least less negative. You can also try to challenge your first thoughts, looking for the counter evidence that something isn't quite so negative.

2. Challenge Your Negative Thoughts

You may find that when you look for evidence that might support your negative thoughts you can't find any. Many negative thoughts are based on our fears. If there is no real evidence, look for other ways to explain

(Continued)

(Continued)

negative events. Even if you do find some evidence, don't assume that's the case. Look for other explanations or reasons.

3. Reframe Negative Events

Look for the silver lining and reframe the event in a positive light. Focus your attention on the positive parts of your life instead of the negative things. You may want to go back to Chapter 6 on reframing.

4. Take Positive Actions

If there is something you can do, do it. In the exercise where you write down all the things that will prevent a good night's sleep, remove the issues about which there is nothing you can do, and focus on the ones that allow you to act. If you get stuck, think smaller. What is one kind thing you can do for someone else right now?

Positivity Is a Choice

It may not be easy to become an optimist if it isn't your nature, but if you want to feel more positive and optimistic, it's worth trying. The first thing you might do to become more positive is to focus on the positive. When you experience a challenge or an obstacle of some kind, don't focus on what is negative. Instead, reframe the negativity by focusing on the positive aspects of your obstacle. Can you learn something from dealing with the challenge? Can you identify the opportunity in the challenge? You will have an easier time coming up with a solution if you are positive.

Have Faith in Yourself

You have overcome challenges in the past, and you will do the same in the future. Believe you will succeed, if not at first, then eventually. Tell yourself you can do anything you put your mind to. You will improve your chances of success by believing in yourself.

Surround Yourself with Positive People

Your parents were right when they criticized the people you hung out with, or maybe that was just me. You are going to be like the people you spend time with. If you were to throw a white handkerchief into a mud puddle, the handkerchief would not turn the water clear. The handkerchief would become dirty. The negative people in your world, especially pessimists, will infect you with their negativity. The opposite is also true. If you want to be positive, optimistic, future-oriented, and empowered, you need to surround yourself with positive people.

Optimism Can Be Developed

Optimism can be developed over time. It will make you happier and provide a more fulfilling life. You can start by looking for the silver lining. Even if something goes wrong, you can still gain something positive. Don't focus on the negative. That is your negativity bias taking hold of you.

Take it away when it isn't helpful. Negative emotions and feelings are normal, but when you can, focus on what is positive. Be patient in your pursuit of positivity, and forgive yourself when you are negative, especially when you should be negative.

There are so many good outcomes that come from being an optimist, starting with improved mental and physical health. It builds resilience too. It can also increase your success in life.

10

Minding Mindfulness

I AM NOT a Zen Buddhist, but I have spent time studying with two Zen masters. Ken Wilber, one of my teachers, and the most cited philosopher in academia in the United States, first introduced me to Genpo Roshi. A *Roshi* is a spiritual leader of Zen Buddhist monks. I spent three days with Genpo Roshi in Salt Lake City to attend an event he was leading.

In 1983, Genpo started studying Voice Dialogue, a Jungian therapeutic technique designed to expand an individual's choices by guiding conscious and intentional behavior. I went to Salt Lake City to experience what Genpo describes as Big Mind, a combination of Eastern Buddhist insight with Western psychoanalytical ideas.

The attendees at this three-day event were Buddhists who had converted because they found it eased their suffering. As a non-Buddhist, I observed Genpo engage people in the Big Mind process over the first day.

It was difficult for some of the participants to practice Big Mind. Genpo would say, "Let me speak to the controller." The person was supposed to respond, "I am the controller" because it makes the person the object of the conversation, not the subject. Most people struggled with this and instead said something like, "Bob is the controller," and Genpo would correct them.

When the person took the voice of the controller, Genpo would ask, "What do you control?" The controller would say, "I control Bob." Genpo would continue, "Why do you have to control Bob?" The controller would answer that if he didn't control Bob, Bob would get himself in all kinds of trouble. In this example, Bob was not speaking for himself. Instead, he was taking a passive role in his life.

At one point on the second day, Genpo asked to speak to my controller. My controller responded for me. Then he asked to speak to the helpless child. The helpless child responded. Then he asked to speak to the Buddha that creates baby buddhas. I had no idea about a Buddha that makes baby buddhas. A few minutes later, I took on the voice of the Buddha that creates baby buddhas, and I experienced something the Buddhists call One Taste. Big Mind made a clearing that allowed me to see something profound, and it lasted for almost two days.

Practicing Mindfulness

When you practice mindfulness, you are the observer, not the subject. You observe sounds, thoughts, feelings, ideas, fears, and that pain in your back. Over time, you realize you are not your thoughts, you are not your feelings, and you are not your ideas. All of these things are simply objects of your mind. You look at them without judging them, and you let them fly by as you are noticing something else.

Genpo told me that I should never spend 40 years sitting on a pillow meditating like he did, even though there was absolutely zero possibility of that happening. He said it is a waste of time. I have practiced meditation for years, following Genpo's recommendation: I sit on a chair with my hands on my legs, observing and noticing what runs through my mind. I don't hold onto anything I notice. This mindfulness practice creates a distance between you and the thoughts that emerge as you are practicing. If you are the kind of person who wakes up in the middle of the night, sit on a chair and cover up with a blanket and meditate. Even if you don't go back to sleep, you'll feel like you slept.

Taming Drunken Monkeys

The Buddha said that human minds are full of drunken monkeys, chattering away, fighting, distracting, and creating chaos in the mind. One of the first things non-meditators worry about is not being able to sit without their mind running wild. The goal in meditation isn't to empty your mind of thoughts, but rather to notice them in the moment. What you are doing is staying in the present moment, even though your drunken monkeys will try to grab your attention and run away with it. Over time, you will be able use the distance between your thoughts and feelings to tame them.

My second Zen master was Doshin Roshi, who helped me practice mindfulness meditation over a couple of months. Zen masters believe that living means knowing you are already dead. This is powerful form of liberation. After we had spent months together, I told him I was no longer afraid of dying, which I had believed to be my greatest fear. Without a second to consider what I had just said, he told me, "That isn't what you are afraid of." I asked him to tell me what he saw so I could see it myself. He said, "You are afraid of being helpless." His assessment was more than accurate. I choked on the idea that I could ever be helpless. I told him that he wasn't coming to save me, but that I was coming to save him. Smiling, he counseled me that I had more work to do to come to grips with the idea that someday I would need help.

You can't always see who and what you are. Some of your best teachers and coaches are the ones who show you something in yourself that you cannot see on your own. Other times you reach this point by practicing mindfulness.

Daily Life with Mindfulness

People who practice transcendental meditation, including Jerry Seinfeld, Oprah, Lady Gaga, David Lynch, and Ray Dalio, swear by it.[1] The strictest adherents commit to two 20-minute sessions each day, but pausing for a brief mindfulness break even every few days can help you be more positive because it provides a number of benefits, including those explained below.

Emotional Regulation

Mindfulness can help you regulate your emotions.[2] In part, I believe it is because you create a distance between yourself and your thoughts. This helps you manage your feelings by giving you more objectivity. It also serves as a reminder that you are not defined by your mood. Rather, you are a being who experiences passing events and emotions; you do not need to carry them with you. For example, I am at my worst when I am tired and frustrated, so I remind myself that my existence is not one of tiredness and frustration. Those are temporary things I experience, but they do not define me. I have practiced meditation enough to know that, as the Buddhists say, "I am perfect exactly as I am, and I can use some improvement." I'll bet you might benefit from a bit of improvement.

Compassion and Self-Compassion

We all need to be compassionate with ourselves and others. Having compassion for others means giving them the benefit of the doubt and acknowledging that all of us experience bad moods, negative emotions, and rough days. Imagine how you've felt on a truly awful day and extend others the kindness that you may have needed at the time.

Self-compassion is just as important and potentially more difficult. You demonstrate self-compassion when you give yourself grace when you are experiencing stress or anxiety. On a daily basis, self-compassion is taking care of your body, mind, and spirit, and bringing balance to your life.

Cognitive Benefits

One of the surprising benefits of mindfulness is better cognition.[3] Maybe by slowing down and putting our drunken monkeys in time out, we think more clearly and creatively.

Stress Reduction

If mindfulness offered only one benefit, this is one that many people would pick. I believe stress and anxiety are so prominent in our environment of accelerating, constant, disruptive change (ACDC) that our educators are starting to teach these stress-reducing strategies to children, and they will need it.[4]

The Importance of Mindfulness

In an article titled "How Mindfulness Can Reshape Negative Thought Patterns," Jason Linder provides a way to escape from negative thought patterns. Linder notes we have 17,000 to 50,000 thoughts each day and 90% of them get repeated.[5] This reinforces the stories we believe about ourselves, even when they are not true. Linder calls these thinking patterns "mental tapes." Mindfulness can have you identify the mental tape and how you acquired it, lessening its hold on your attention.

Yogi Alina Prax describes it this way:

Most of the time, we don't even know we're breathing. We breathe automatically and without notice. Switching over to a conscious breathing pattern instantly changes everything. We become mindful of our breath, and in doing so, we begin to relieve the kind of anxiety that accompanies an unaware way of moving through the world. Many of us have an unhealthy pattern of holding our breath—especially when we're stressed.[6]

I have a bookmark to an article on Mindfulness.com called "4 Steps to Overcome Negative Thoughts."[7] It reminds me that I am not trying to remove my negative thoughts and emotions. Instead, the goal is to label them, a technique called Name It to Tame It. Naming sources of negativity can reduce the power of the thoughts and emotions it feeds.[8]

This book relies on a lot of science, but my goals is to write something practical and full of easy-to-use strategies. However, some research is worth exploring more deeply. In "Integrating Mindfulness into Positive Psychology: a Randomised Controlled Trial of an Online Positive Mindfulness Program," researchers describe the effects of eight-week online positive mindfulness program based on intervention techniques. Before the program, participants were measured in gratitude, self-compassion, self-efficacy, meaning, and autonomy. Then participants in the experimental group completed the positive mindfulness program, while participants in the control group did not. After the program, both groups were measured again on the same traits. The results: The group that had gone through the positive mindfulness program scored significantly higher in all measures than the control group. One month after the program ended, the experimental group participants still reported higher scores than the control group, a sign that the benefits of mindfulness can be long lasting.[9]

You may have come across the phrase "don't just do something, sit there." There is evidence that mindfulness has benefits for mental and physical health. It can reduce stress and anxiety, lessen depression, and improve sleep. But it also can lead to greater focus, better concentration, and even an immune-system boost. And mindfulness can come from a variety of methods, including yoga, meditation, contemplative prayer, journaling, or simply paying attention to the present moment.

An Easy Way to Practice Mindfulness

You know those snow globes people bring out at Christmas? Your mind resembles those snow globes with all kinds of things going this way and that. When you mediate, you allow the blizzard in your mind to settle, and your negativity falls away along with everything else, giving you an opportunity to connect with yourself.

If you have never mediated and would like some help, there are plenty of apps that offer more structure, including activities and guided sessions. Headspace, Calm, and the Healthy Minds Program are three reputable apps that can get you started. (The first two are about $70 per year, and the Healthy Minds Program is free). I like Headspace, which was created by a Buddhist-monk-turned-entrepreneur. Each meditation session explains what you are supposed to be doing, so you don't get distracted wondering *Am I doing this right?* There are little animations that explain the concepts, making it easy to follow along. You can start with a five-minute guided meditation, then increase the length of your sessions as you develop your practice.

You can also go to YouTube and find all kinds of guided meditations in different lengths and focuses, like sleep, anxiety, and beginning meditation. Remember that longer isn't necessarily better.

Following is a list of strategies for practicing mindfulness.

Focus on Your Breath

I had no idea what I was doing when I started to practice mindfulness, but it turns out to be as simple as breathing. To use this strategy, sit comfortably, close your eyes, and pay attention to your breath coming in and going out. For years this was the only kind of mindfulness practice I did, and I was eventually able to sit for long periods of time only paying attention to my breathing. Doshin Roshi told me I was practicing samadhi, an intense concentration, which is one way to cultivate mindfulness.

Scan Your Body

A body scan is a kind of meditation that focuses on your physical vessel as a way to clear your mind and shift your attention. While sitting or lying in a comfortable position, you start by focusing on one part of your body, typically the toes or the head, and noticing any sensations like tension, comfort, pain, or warmth. Move your attention slowly along your body, focusing on each part as you go. For my money, I start at the top of my head and move down. If you are noticing, you are on the right track.

Mindfulness in Ordinary Activities

The Buddhists have a saying: "Before enlightenment, chop wood, wash dishes. After enlightenment, chop wood, wash dishes." This is something akin to "How you do one thing is how you do everything." Your subconscious mind can brush your teeth and drive you to work without your full attention. Instead of being on autopilot, notice what you're doing, including your sensations and your thoughts in the moment. You can do this with anything you do throughout your day.

Nonjudgmental Observations

Your mind judges things to decide how you should respond. Mindfulness challenges you to observe things without judgment so you can achieve an inner peace and acceptance. The world's greatest samurai, Miyamoto Musashi, wrote a list of 21 precepts for life. The first is, "Accept everything as it is." That means no judgment.

The Science of Mindfulness

It turns out that there has been extensive research on mindfulness.[10] It can help alleviate pain and increase trait mindfulness and psychological health.[11] It can also help you manage stress and reduce your burnout,[12] but for our purposes here, mindfulness has been known to lower levels of repetitive negative thinking.[13] I will offer only one recommendation: If you are not a meditator, pick up an app and start practicing mindfulness, if only to reduce your negative thoughts. You can't get this wrong.

11

How to Forget Your Problems and Concerns

IMAGINE YOU ARE upset, anxious, or angry. Your inner narrative has done an exceptional job helping you become negative. You struggle to release yourself from your negativity because you can't afford to remain in this state; you have work to do and you have a family that needs you to feed them and spend time with them without being negative. There is a strategy that can release you from this suffering: helping a person who needs help. Go to the grocery store and take a bag of food to your local pantry. Take balloons to a retirement home and visit with the people who live there. Bring a plate of cookies to the new mother who already has a large brood and could use a little help.

As soon as we start helping others, we lose our concern for ourselves. Even if the effects last only for a short while, it's fascinating to experience. Humans need others—families, villages, tribes, neighbors, and our modern communities—to thrive and flourish, and being a part of that can liberate us from our own negative feelings.

In a shopping center in New York City, a woman collapsed onto the floor. We happened to be very near her, and Cher, being a nurse, immediately started taking care of her. A minute or two later, two more people asked what they could do, and Cher sent them to get help. Eventually, a few other people showed up to see what they could do. Eventually, a paramedic showed up and treated her. The poor woman had heat stroke and didn't need all the attention, but she was grateful for the help. It is difficult to feel negative when you are focusing on helping others.

Why I Buy All the Dogs

You don't need to help a person for this strategy to remove your negative state. Caring for any sentient being can bring the same effects. For a few years, I have walked into the Delaware County Humane Society and bought all the dogs. It may sound ridiculous, but I don't take the dogs home. I already have two dogs and two cats living in my house, and we are happy with that situation. But on occasion, I am a sort of amateur bail bondsman for dogs, paying their adoption fees so they can more easily find forever homes. The last time I bought all the dogs, the people working at the Humane Society asked me if they could use the money to pay for any training or other services some of the animals needed. I agreed and paid for nine dogs, a little over $1,200.

The day after I bought the nine dogs, the Delaware County Humane Society posted about the advance-paid adoption fees and included a picture of me sitting with a big white pit bull. After reading the story, one woman went to the shelter and paid for all the cats. There had to be more than 100 of them! Buying all the dogs certainly made me feel happy and reminded me that I can have a positive impact on the world, but seeing it inspire someone else was almost as good a feeling. It's a good example of how taking one simple action can reverberate across the lives of others.

Why Give to the Homeless

I started giving money to homeless people when I lived in Los Angeles. One day, as I was walking to the grocery store, a homeless man lying next to a dumpster started yelling to me as I passed him. He had noticed my waist-length hair, so he pulled out his guitar and asked me to sing a song with him. I told him, "Maybe next time." He said there wasn't going to be a next time and introduced himself as Happy Trails. He asked me for money, and I said no, explaining that I knew he would use it to buy wine. He countered that if it would make him happy, why would I deprive him. After this encounter, I started giving homeless people money without worrying about what they'd do with it.

One night after going out to dinner with my wife and one of my daughters, we pulled up to a traffic light. I noticed a man standing on the corner in the pouring rain. It was so dark, I could hardly see him. I got out of the car and gave him the $80 I had in cash. The man turned his back to us, ashamed that we were watching him count the money. When he turned back around, he was crying. He yelled, "I can go home! I can go home!" My daughter asked me why I gave him the money and how I knew he wasn't planning to use it to buy drugs or alcohol. I told her I didn't give him money to control him, but because I could.

I wrote about this story in a newsletter, and not too long after, one of my clients walked past a homeless man and his dog at a truck stop. My client offered to pay for a shower and a meal. The homeless man rejected the offer because he couldn't leave his dog alone. My client said he would sit with the dog, which the stranger was uncomfortable with at first. After all, who would leave their pet with a stranger. But he eventually accepted the money and took a shower and bought food for himself and his dog. My client cried while telling this story in front of 50 of his peers. He said, "I am ashamed that I walked past these people before reading your story." That's when the rest of us started tearing up.

My theory about why we had an emotional response when my client shared that he was ashamed of his prior behavior is because is because we all have walked past people who have needed our help. Acting in those situations is a powerful form of empathy and compassion.

Some people wonder why I do these things, and I know it's because of my mother, a single mom raising four kids who was also incredibly charitable. She is my role model, even though I will never come close to matching her impact. When we were young, my mother somehow found out that the Italian woman who lived in the apartment behind us didn't have any money to buy her three children Christmas presents. Even though we didn't have much money either, my mother found a way to buy all of them presents and food. Under the cover of night, we delivered the presents. This instinct to help people is a family trait. My grandmother was also a single mother of four sons and one daughter, and she would feed anyone who needed dinner. A year after I had brain surgery, my grandmother also had a small brain surgery, but that didn't stop her from cooking her fried chicken for the family—and ending my time as a vegetarian.

Helper's High

Helping others can take you from negative to positive by improving your sense of well-being and happiness. We are social creatures; we need other people, and they need us. While helping others can give our self-esteem and self-worth a boost, I believe that our empathy and compassion stem from recognizing that, at times, we need help from others. It may also be a form of reciprocity in reverse; we help, hoping others will help us.

There is something called the helper's high. Not to worry—it's safe and you don't need a medical card. When we help others, our bodies create mood-boosting endorphins and release the hormone oxytocin, which promotes trust, empathy, and stress reduction. Helping others also causes our brains to release dopamine, a neurotransmitter that triggers feelings of pleasure. This provides positive reinforcement that can encourage us to help others in the future. This type of prosocial behavior supplies all the benefits of endorphins and dopamine without the risks of more artificial addictive behaviors.

Certain addictive behaviors, like drug use or scrolling through social media, can flood your brain with dopamine. Regularly triggering intense spikes of dopamine can overwhelm your brain, which tries to adapt by changing its structure and reducing the number of dopamine receptor cells. As a result, people find that it's harder to feel pleasure or joy without engaging in their addictive behavior because they need that massive surge of dopamine.[1] Social media companies have confessed they use this dopamine feedback loop to get people to spend more time on their platforms.[2] In other words, social media is engineered to be addictive.

If you want to boost your self-esteem and dopamine, choose kindness and prosocial behavior. When you help others you prove that you see and value them. Carry cash with you so you can take advantage of the opportunity to help someone who needs it. For a few donated dollars, you can buy yourself a helper's high that brings better mental health, improved physical health, and stronger connections to others.

This strategy can be especially beneficial when you are facing problems, so on tough days, take a break to do something nice for someone else. I promise that your problems will be waiting for you when you return, and your improved mood and reduced stress might help you find a solution more easily than trying to push through a haze of stress. And remember, you have shelter, food, high-speed internet, and people who love you, so things may not be as bad as they seem.

I believe we are here to make a positive difference, no matter how small or how large. For one activity at Harvard Business School, I was matched with an entrepreneur from the Philippines, which was facing a food crisis and starvation was a real risk. My partner went to China and secured a hearty breed of corn that could grow more easily in the Philippine climate, saving hundreds of thousands of lives. I helped tens of thousands of people to get work, not coming close to the reach my teammate made by winning clients that provided my company the ability to provide work. He did what he could with his resources; I did what I could with mine.

Do This Now

Each of us can help where and when we can. You and I can make a difference and spread greater positivity in a world with more than enough negativity. Look at the following list of ideas, and consider what you can do today:

- Donate to an animal shelter.
- Volunteer at a homeless shelter or soup kitchen.
- Get some friends, family members, or neighbors together to engage in an informal food drive.

- Contact a local woman's shelter and find out how to donate money or clothing.
- Leave a bag of groceries on the front porch of someone in need.
- Volunteer to teach children to read.
- Bring books or toys to a children's hospital.

Before we start your Negativity Fast, I need to make a confession. Part of the reason I wrote this book was to help people feel better. As a reader, I talk about books with other people all the time, and one thing that strikes me is how many people read a book, then stick it on the shelf and continue their lives as before. Reading a book without using the new information and strategies you acquire is a waste. If you don't apply what you read to your life, it's as though you never read the book. Keep this in mind after you read *The Negativity Fast* so you can act on what you learn and change the rhythm of your life.

Altruism Is Important to Society

Altruism is important for our society because it helps us cooperate with each other and connect around a shared moral value, regardless of what we have or what help we need. Not only is altruism good for society and people who need help, but doing good deeds is also good for you when it comes to being positive. There are plenty of ways to contribute by helping others, including the following.

You: Philanthropist

You don't have to be a Buffett, a Walton, or a Bezos to be a philanthropist. In fact, sharing what you can with others may feel more costly to you because you may not have a few hundred million you can spare. Even so, your contribution helps others while also benefiting you by making you feel good and positive.

The Most Expensive Gift: Volunteering

Money is easier to give than time because your time is a finite resource. But the time you provide as a volunteer brings you a return in the form of emotional benefits like increased happiness, life satisfaction, and a decrease in depression.

Small Acts of Kindness

There is no reason to believe that you don't have enough to give. A small act of kindness feels bigger to the person that receives your generosity because it shows that someone cares about them. When I bought the nine dogs, it had a ripple effect because it inspired someone else to do something similar, which could have encouraged someone else to do something generous. This plays out every day on a large and small scale. For instance, my friend Lisa needed a kidney and a stranger donated one. That is an impressive act of altruism, and it could have had a long-reaching effect by reshuffling the donor-match list.

Paying It Forward

The Universe is strange place. You never have to do anything with the expectation of reciprocity because kindness brings you immense benefits. Someday you may need help, so you can pay it forward today. It feels good to be able to do something for someone else.

Tamping Down Your Negativity Bias

To tamp down your negativity bias, all you need to do is to find someone who needs a helping hand. I believe that this is true because you are no longer thinking about yourself.

The Science of Helping Others

In a paper titled "When Helping Helps: Autonomous Motivation for Prosocial Behavior and Its Influence on Well-Being for the Helper and Recipient," the researchers suggest that "autonomous helping" can improve the well-being of the person being helped and the helper by alleviating stress and negative mental states.[3]

There is a downside in some scenarios. Leaders who help followers with personal problems can cause a negative effect, especially when they help with task-based problems.[4] This means the leader has a negative effect from helping. The paper suggests that when prosocial impact is high, the negative effect is less.[5]

The next time you are negative, find an opportunity to help someone and offer to help them. There is no end of people and causes that deserve attention. There is a homeless shelter that needs a volunteer and money. There is a pantry that needs groceries. There is a church or a charity close enough that you could support. Or if you have two hours, you can give platelets to the Red Cross and help people with cancer. One person in one of my businesses grows his hair out so he can give it to people with cancer. If you are the kind of person who would read a book like this one, I am certain you can come up with something you can do to help others, even though you will also be the beneficiary of your help.

12

The Negativity Fast

IT'S NOW TIME to prepare to start your Negativity Fast. The chapters you finished have prepared you to complete your fast successfully. By understanding your negativity, you gain power over it. Each of the chapters has covered internal sources of negativity, like your self-talk, complaining, and being ungrateful.

At some point after you finish a fast or two, you will find you are not nearly as easy to trigger. You may find that you want to continue certain parts of your fast, maybe forever. For me, I avoid politics and the overly political. After 90 days of no politics, I walked through an airport and walked right past the television broadcasting CNN with no interest in whatever the talking heads were arguing about.

Before we start, I want you to know that you may break your fast. The world brings all kinds of surprises, including negative surprises. Remember, the goal here is not to be negative when situations call for negativity. The goal is to remove the sources of negativity that poison your mindset and reduce the quality of your life.

When—not if—you go straight negative, just pick up where you left off and carry on. Remember, you are a biopsychosocialspiritual entity, which is to say you are complex and complicated. At the beginning of the book, I gave you permission to be negative when it is the right response.

Over the course of 90 days, focus on eliminating as many sources of negativity as possible. Replace it with something positive. Don't overthink it; just avoid negativity however it shows up in your world. We can often be the biggest sources of negativity for ourselves, so don't forget to look at your own behaviors, thought patterns, and habits. Most of all, remember that your beliefs cause your negativity, not the activating event.

Identify the Sources of Negativity

The first thing you need to do to prepare for your Negativity Fast is to identify the sources of your negativity and write them down on your trigger list. Importantly, do *not* include people in your life, no matter how irksome they may be, until the very end of this process. They'll be the last thing on your trigger list.

To prepare your trigger list, consider the things that people complain about most, keeping in mind that some triggers are difficult to avoid. Include those persistent triggers on your list, along with the minor irritations in your life. You are now armed with strategies for dealing with all of them. Since preparation is so important, each item on your trigger list should also include a note about how you will avoid it. That way, you don't have to come up with a strategy on the spot. I'll go first and share my triggers.

Politics and the Overly Political

For some reason, some people believe they are going to change other people's politics—and they put a lot of effort into arguing with people who have different opinions. I was once one of those people who found their identity in politics, so I can understand what it feels like to be consumed by ideology. When people are overly political, they tend to be negative about half their country, including family members and friends who see things differently. There are a number of things you can do instead of being baited into a political argument. First, you can avoid these people, but if that isn't possible, you can always bow out politely by saying, "I am not up to speed on this issue; thanks for sharing that with me." Then walk away—fast.

Eliminating your exposure to political media and social media is relatively easy. Remove those apps and accounts from your phone; unsubscribe from political newsletters, emails, and publications; and don't turn on cable news for the duration of your Negativity Fast. We're not including people on your trigger list, but you probably have a few in mind. Instead, avoid particular political topics that tend to make you negative. Everyone has some hot-button issue that can get them going, so acknowledge yours and avoid all discussion of it. As for overly political people, keep your distance for the next 90 days. This doesn't mean you need to ignore them entirely, but don't get bogged down in a conversation about politics. Change the subject, excuse yourself, and go talk to someone more positive. By the time you finish your Negativity Fast, this will be easier, and you will be harder to trigger.

Global Issues

Geopolitics—things like wars, famines, the increasing number of autocrats taking power across our world—is closely related to overly political news, but it tends to unfold with a little more distance than daily Red State–versus–Blue State battles. You will feel more negative if you obsess over all the things going wrong that you cannot change. Acknowledge these things and let them go. This doesn't mean you need to stop being concerned; it just means you need to keep things in perspective. If you care about some issue, send money to the causes you believe in but don't focus your mental and emotional energy dwelling on these issues. If you choose to stay informed, pick up a moderate news source like the *Economist* and limit the amount of time you spend following these stories for the next 90 days. Once you have a greater immunity to being triggered, you can go back to paying attention to these things.

Media Triggers

This is one area you will need to do some pruning. First, consume no news. No local new shows. No morning shows with people sitting around a table talking about politics or gossiping. Absolutely no cable news shows, regardless of their political bent. Also, no media about movie stars or television stars. If you must drive to work, use that time to listen to something positive, something we will work on later.

Existential Dread

The threat of nuclear weapons and fears about the climate make for seriously powerful triggers for a lot of people. Only one of my three children wants to have children; the other two worry about the world not being a good place and believe it is wrong to add to the global population. This planet has never been without its threats, and human beings march forward, despite the risks.

In addition to writing down your triggers, this is an opportunity to create a second list of everything you love about living on Planet Earth. The reason I remind people about the 4,108 weeks they have been gifted is to remind them that they have already punched their ticket, so they may as well make it count.

Weather and Other Natural Occurrences

I live in Ohio where the sky is gray for half the year. If you don't like the weather in Ohio, you need only wait 12 hours for the temperature to swing roughly 50 degrees. Tennessee and Oklahoma have tornados, Florida and a large part of the lower South have hurricanes, and California has fires, mudslides, and earthquakes. The West doesn't have enough water. During hurricane season, the East Coast gets too much.

If weather is a trigger, you really need a Negativity Fast. What he failed to mention is that there is no place with perfect weather and no natural disasters. You may be better off recognizing the awesome power of nature.

Transportation Inconveniences

Whether you are flying, traveling by train, or driving home from work, you can do more productive things than complain. Let's say you have a 45-minute drive time; you can claim that time to do something you enjoy, like listening to a sports channel, your favorite podcast, some music you love, or an audiobook (like *The Negativity Fast*).

Make a list of the things you can do that will be valuable to you while you are stuck in traffic or experiencing a delay at the airport or train station. Make sure you have sources you can turn to when you need to shift from negative to positive.

Money, Taxes, and Inflation

We live in an economic world. If you believe money issues were better in the past, you are mistaken. Money is necessary to life, and for all our time on this planet, people have had to find a way to take care of shelter, heat, food, high-speed internet, DoorDash, and Netflix. Pay your taxes, save us much as you can, and do your best not to obsess about money. The research suggests that once you have a certain amount of money, more money won't make you any happier.[1]

The only advice I can offer is that creating a list of your expenses and working out a budget can help you avoid the problems that cause negativity around money. If you have trouble sticking to your budget, see what you can live without. You'll find that there are plenty of free and low-cost ways to spend your time, especially through volunteering opportunities or outdoor recreation.

Health Issues and Lack of Sleep

Your physical and mental health are critical to living a good and productive life. We don't always take care of ourselves because we tell ourselves we are too busy, but our health is *the* major factor in our well-being.

Make two lists here, starting with the excuses you use to avoid taking care of yourself. For example, many people who are prescribed medicines fail to take them faithfully.[2] When it comes to consistently taking medication, some people take better care of their pets than they do of themselves.[3,4] The second list should include what you are going to do to take better care of yourself. Pretend that you are someone you love, and give yourself the same level of attention and care.

Lack of Time

One of my affirmations each day is: "I have enough time." This is a positive lie I tell myself, and it is starting to stick, even though I know I have the same 24 hours as everyone else. This affirmation is the result of being stretched. There are any number of reasons you feel a lack of time, including taking on too many projects, being disorganized, and lacking a plan for your week. If you take on more tasks than you can handle at one time, you are one of my tribe.

First start by making a list of the reasons you are time-starved and add a list of behavioral changes will need to make. Then make a weekly calendar and populate it with your real and most important priorities, starting with your health and your relationships.

Work Issues and Other Triggers

Work often comes with conflict, whether clients or the people you work with every day. This can be difficult, and you may not be able to avoid the tasks and situations that trigger your negativity. Do your best to limit your exposure to the most negative people at your workplace. In a meeting, draw a happy face on your legal pad and write down anything someone says that is negative and, after the meeting, cross it out.

Trivialities

I am afraid I can't write this list for you. I can only give my list of trivial triggers that I have to work to overcome.

You will need to make your own list of the little things that you make into big things.

- **Administrative work or any form I am required to complete.** My inner voice tells me that people are stealing my time, the only finite, nonrenewable commodity we have. To deal with my negativity around administrative work, I started Financial Friday, doing all the paperwork that comes into my life just one day a week. It normally only takes me a couple of hours, and I feel better when it is done.
- **Noise pollution.** You might think that someone who was once the front man for a rock 'n' roll group should be able to deal with noise pollution, having created it in the past. A few years ago, I bought a very expensive pair of Bang & Olufsen over-ear headphones that I keep with me, because the announcements on an airplane are delivered through a speaker directly above your head. Problem solved.
- **Potholes:** You might think this is something too little to trigger negativity. After four tire replacements in two months, it became a trigger. I took the car back to the dealer and asked them to buy the car back. I left with a car that didn't have poor tires and soft wheels. During the writing of this book, I hit a serious pothole that ruptured my tire, and I changed my route to avoid more damage.
- **I have self-diagnosed myself with misophonia.** I apologize in advance if this triggers you. Misophonia is when you are triggered by noises made when someone is eating. It's gross. I confess I haven't yet found the answer to this trigger.

- **The scam telemarketers who try to steal your credit card.** This no longer triggers me. Instead of being angry, I try encouraging the person on the phone to go find a job that doesn't require them to harm other people. I also tell them their mother is worried about them and that they should go see her after work.

Negative People

We need to take a careful view of people triggers. It's important to recognize that, from time to time, you trigger people, and people also trigger you. We need to start by being empathetic, because we are all part of the family that is humanity.

There are some people you know who are super negative; you may even love some of them. Others you might see only on holidays. As much as you can, try to stay away from negative people while you are on your Negativity Fast. This includes complainers, the ungrateful, gossips, and teenagers (teenagers are negative by default). In addition to the typical whiners, stupid people are one of my triggers, a quality I probably share with many people. In a tiny book titled *The Basic Laws of Human Stupidity*, the third basic law states, "A stupid person is a person who causes a loss to another person or to a group of persons while himself deriving no gain and even possibly incurring losses."[5]

This definition is important in helping you limit your exposure to a kind of person who might trigger your negativity. Did this person cause you some loss? If not, they are probably not stupid.

In fact, most people are not stupid. They are, however, negative, fearful, anxious, occasionally clumsy, negligent, overwhelmed, and distracted. Most are doing their best, even if they cause problems.

You trigger yourself when you assign motivations to people without knowing or understanding the real reason they did something that inconvenienced you or worse. It's important to go back and remind yourself that the activating event is not the reason you are triggered. Your belief about the event and what it means is you triggering you.

Identifying the Sources of Positivity

When I did my first Negativity Fast, I made a huge mistake. While I eliminated all the negative sources in my life, I didn't replace them with anything positive. At one point, I thought to myself that my mind had been poisoned with negativity over the course of my life, with a glass as the metaphor for my mind. I decided that I needed a pressure hose of positivity to blast out the negativity that had accumulated. Over the next 60 days I listened to everything Steven Covey published, followed by Earl Nightingale, Anthony Robbins, Les Brown, Peter Drucker, guided meditations, *The Four Agreements*, Jim Rohn, Tom Peters, and Ken Wilber. Over time, I've expanded the list to include Mel Robbins, Lewis Howes, Jay Shetty, Brendon Burchard, Brené Brown, Darren Hardy, Anthony Robbins, Jocko Willink, and Ryan Holiday.

You may have other positive sources. When you are in the shower, driving to work, taking the kids to school or to dance recitals, you have time to listen to an audio program or a positive podcast. The more you feed your mind with positivity, the more time you will spend in a positive state, meaning less time in negative states.

Your People

In a wonderful book titled *The Art of Gathering: How We Meet and Why It Matters* by Priya Parker, the author argues that gathering is much more than a way to get together.[6] Instead, people build community, share meaning, and solve problems, among other positive outcomes. Those of us with large families and a lot of friends have an easier time gathering everyone together, even if we aren't making a difference in the world outside of our world. Every month, more than 50 of us gather to celebrate the people with birthdays, sometimes colliding into Easter, Mother's Day, Father's Day, Halloween, Thanksgiving, Christmas, or New Year's, plus football games, boxing, or some other reason to get together.

You belong to these people, and they belong to you, even the difficult family members. You have friends you haven't seen in a long while, and they would love to spend time with you. As I write this, I just took a call from one of my best friends, Larry, who I've been close to since I was 13 years old. He is now recovered from open-heart surgery and back to work at the firehouse. We used his windshield time to catch up over half an hour I was supposed to be working. Larry was more important. I fed him when he ran away from home, which meant camping. When I ran away from home and drove an El Camino to Naples, Florida, he ratted me out because he didn't like the person I went with.

Your Priorities

Ben Franklin said, "Old too soon and wise to late." It's easy to focus on your job and making money while ignoring the more important things in life, all of them people and the experiences you share with them. One of my favorite books is *Chasing Daylight* by Eugene O'Kelly, who was the CEO of KPMG. One day he discovered he had an aggressive brain cancer called glioblastoma. There is no treatment. O'Kelly decided not to waste his last six months. He drew five concentric circles, the largest being the tens of thousands who worked for him. He was going to work his way to the smallest circle, his immediate family. About halfway through his plan to spend the end of his life with his family, he realized he made a mistake, noting he should have sent a letter and spent his remaining time with his family. You and I are also chasing daylight. If you want to mediate on your priorities, know that it is people.

Pursuing Joy

Most of the time, you should try to find joy. In your work. In your home. In your family and friends. And in what you do every day. I am a writer, and Cher supports me sitting in my office typing (badly) and increasing my carpal tunnel that I will need to address.

Journal Your Negative and Positive States

One way to keep track of your Negativity Fast is to keep a journal. At some point, you will find yourself in a negative space. Write down what you were thinking and what triggered the negativity. You want to keep a list of these events so you can deal with them effectively in the future. Remember, you are allowed to be negative. The goal isn't to never be negative or experience a foul mood. The goal is to be less negative and more positive more of the time. No judgment when you are negative but do notice it and make notes about what is going on. Write it down and capture it on paper, reducing its power over you.

Also write in your journal any time you are positive, optimistic, and empowered. One reason to note these positive events and feelings is that it causes you to notice the good things and feels. What was going on that helped put you in a positive place? When something causes you to be more positive, do more of it. If certain people lift your mood, spend more time with them (my guess is that these are positive friends). This will be a journal of your Negativity Fast and what you learned about yourself.

It can help to track your habits, starting with sleep, hydration, exercise, and diet. These simple things can have an outsized impact on your state. You can buy a habit tracker journal or draw little check boxes to keep track of these things. I use the Apple Watch to track my sleep because I am trying to improve the time I spend in deep sleep. (I am not doing very well at this yet.) I also log my water intake each day.

What to Do When You Fall Off the Horse

You may fall off the horse. You were angry, and you lost it. It happens to the most positive people you know because they are human. Just pick up where you left off or start fresh tomorrow morning after a good night's sleep. Don't believe that you somehow failed. It's impossible for you to fail because you were not seeking perfection. You were pursuing feeling more positive more of the time and reducing your negativity. If you have experienced being more positive, you have reached your goal.

Stay the Course and Double Down

Having done the Negativity Fast myself, I can tell you that over time, you may decide that you can give up the sources of your negativity. I never argue with people about politics. I never ingest negativity, whether it comes from the media or from other people or sources.

After you finish your Negativity Fast, you don't have to go back to ingesting negativity. You know that the bad news and negative people will still be there being negative and feeding you their fears. If you feel better, what sense does it make to go back to being negative more of their time? There is no end of people who will happily tell you all about the bad things going on in the world.

I am optimistic that you will succeed and finish your Negativity Fast. I believe you will feel better about your world and your life. You will gain control over your self-talk, have more empathy for other people who may have triggered you in the past, complain a lot less often, be more grateful for what you have, reframe your negative events, live happily despite our politics, look at social media differently, change your negative state when you need to, help others who need it, and, I hope, remove a large part of your negativity.

Any time you start to find yourself feeling negative, stressed, or anxious, restart your Negativity Fast. I liked my first fast well enough that I did two more times in a row. And if you need additional help, please join us at www.negativityfast.com.

Endnotes

Chapter 1: Why You Are Negative

1. Leahy, R. (2002). "Pessimism and the Evolution of Negativity," *Journal of Cognitive Psychotherapy* 16(3): 295–316, doi: 10.1891/jcop.16.3.295.52520.
2. Hasyim, M. (2022). "Why Do Social Media Make People Feel Lonelier Instead of Connecting with Them?" *Technoarete Transactions on Advances in Social Sciences and Humanities* 1(2), https://doi.org/10.36647/ttassh/02.01.a005.
3. Yang, P. (2023). "Relationship Between Social Media and Cyberbullying," *Lecture Notes in Education Psychology and Public Media* 1(5): 812–817, https://doi.org/10.54254/2753-7048/5/2022945.
4. Zyoud, S., Sweileh, W., Awang, R., and Al-Jabi, S. (2018). "Global Trends in Research Related to Social Media in Psychology: Mapping and Bibliometric Analysis," *International Journal of Mental Health Systems* 1(12), https://doi.org/10.1186/s13033-018-0182-6.
5. Hill, W., et al. (2019). "Genetic Contributions to Two Special Factors of Neuroticism Are Associated with Affluence, Higher Intelligence, Better Health, and Longer Life," *Molecular Psychiatry* 11(25): 3034–3052, https://doi.org/10.1038/s41380-019-0387-3.

6. Magal, N., Hendler, T., and Admon, R. (2021). "Is Neuroticism Really Bad for You? Dynamics in Personality and Limbic Reactivity Prior to, During and Following Real-life Combat Stress. Neurobiology of Stress," *Neurobiology of Stress* 15, 100361, https://doi.org/10.1016/j.ynstr.2021.100361.

7. Hoppu, U., Puputti, S., Mattila, S., Puurtinen, M., and Sandell, M. (2020). "Food Consumption and Emotions at a Salad Lunch Buffet in a Multisensory Environment," *Foods* 10(9): 1349, https://doi.org/10.3390/foods9101349.

8. Vanhaecke, T., Bretin, O., Poirel, M., and Tap, J. (2002). "Drinking Water Source and Intake Are Associated with Distinct Gut Microbiota Signatures in US and UK Populations," *Journal of Nutrition* 152(1, Jan 11): 171–182, doi: https://pubmed.ncbi.nlm.nih.gov/34642755/.

9. Mickelson, C., et al. (2020). "Sleep Duration and Subjective Resilience to Sleep Loss Predict Functional Impairment in Elite Infantrymen During Military Training. Sleep," *Supplement* 1(43): A74–A75, https://doi.org/10.1093/sleep/zsaa056.187.

10. Centers for Disease Control and Prevention. (2022). "Benefits of Physical Activity," https://www.cdc.gov/physicalactivity/basics/pa-health/index.htm.

11. Rozin, P., and Royzman, E. B. (2001). "Negativity Bias, Negativity Dominance, and Contagion," *Personality and Social Psychology Review* 5(4): 296–320, https://doi.org/10.1207/S15327957PSPR0504_2.

12. McIntyre, K. (2020). "Tell Me Something Good: Testing the Longitudinal Effects of Constructive News Using the Google Assistant," *Electronic News* 1(14): 37–54, https://doi.org/10.1177/1931243120910446.

Chapter 2: Talking Yourself into a Negative State

1. Robinson, K. (2007). "Do Schools Kill Creativity?" TED, https://youtu.be/iG9CE55wbtY.

2. Kross, E. (2021). *Chatter: The Voice in Our Head, Why It Matters, and How to Harness It*. New York: Crown, p. 34.

3. Albin, J., and Bailey, E. (2021). *Idiot's Guides Cognitive Behavioral Therapy*. New York: Penguin Random House, pp. 103–108.
4. Kross, Chatter, p. 105.
5. Cohen, G. L., and Sherman, D. K. (2014). "The Psychology of Change: Self-Affirmation and Social Psychological Intervention," *Annual Review of Psychology* 65(1): 333–371.
6. Olés, P., Brinhaupt, T. M., Dier, R., and Polak, D. (2020). "Types of Inner Dialogues and Functions of Self-Talk: Comparisons and Implications," *Front. Psychol.* 11(Mar 6): 227, https://doi.org/10.3389/fpsyg.2020.00227.
7. Ibid.

Chapter 3: Empathy and How to Lie to Yourself

1. Salmela, M., and Nagatsu, M. (2017). "How Does It Really Feel to Act Together? Shared Emotions and the Phenomenology of We-Agency," *Phenomenology and the Cognitive Sciences* 16(3): 449–470, https://philpapers.org/rec/SALHDI.
2. Niezink, L., et al. (2012). "Empathic Concern: Distinguishing between Tenderness and Sympathy," *Motivation and Emotion* 36(4), 544–549, https://www.ncbi.nlm.nih.gov/pmc/articles/PMC3491184/.
3. Rolston, A., and Lloyd-Richardson, E. (n.d.) "What Is Emotion Regulation and How Do We Do It?" Cornell Research Program on Self-Injury and Recovery, https://selfinjury.bctr.cornell.edu/perch/resources/what-is-emotion-regulationsinfo-brief.pdf
4. Ellis, A., and Lange, A. (1994). *How to Keep People from Pushing Your Buttons*. New York: Citadel Press, p. 12.
5. Ruiz, D. M. (1997). *The Four Agreements: A Practical Guide to Personal Freedom*. San Rafael, CA: Amber-Allen Publishing.
6. Ge, Y., Li, W., Chen, F., Kayani, S., and Qin, G. (2021). "The Theories of the Development of Students: A Factor to Shape Teacher Empathy from the Perspective of Motivation," *Frontiers in Psychology* 12, https://doi.org/10.3389/fpsyg.2021.736656.
7. Linehan, M. (2021). "Marsha Linehan on radical acceptance," Kinsale CBT, https://www.kinsalecbt.com/2021/01/14/marsha-linehan-on-radical-acceptance/.

8. Trust for America's Health. (2022). "Pain in the Nation: The Epidemics of Alcohol, Drug, and Suicide Deaths 2022," https://www.tfah.org/report-details/pain-in-the-nation-2022/

9. Bieberstein, F., Essl, A., and Friedrich, K. (2021). "Empathy: A Clue for Prosocialty and Driver of Indirect Reciprocity." *PLoS ONE* 8(16), e0255071, https://doi.org/10.1371/journal.pone.0255071.

10. Ibid.

11. Ibid.

12. Wang, S., et al. (2021). "The Hidden Danger in Family Environment: The Role of Self-Reported Parenting Style in Cognitive and Affective Empathy Among Offenders." *Frontiers in Psychology* 12, https://www.frontiersin.org/articles/10.3389/fpsyg.2021.588993/full.

Chapter 4: How to Stop Complaining

1. Choraria, S. (2013). "Exploring the Role of Negative Emotions On Customer's Intention to Complain," *Vision* 3(17), 201–211, https://doi.org/10.1177/0972262913496725.

2. Aubé, C., and Rousseau, V. (2016). "Yes, We Complain . . . So What?" *Journal of Managerial Psychology* 7(31), 1137–1151, https://doi.org/10.1108/jmp-08-2015-0304.

3. Haider, A., and Asad, U. (2018). "Frequency of Somatic Complains Among Patients with Mental Illness," *Annals of Psychophysiology* 1(5): 6–16, https://doi.org/10.29052/2412-3188.v5.i1.2018.6-16.

4. Held, B., and Bohart, A. (2002). "Introduction: The (Overlooked) Virtues of 'Unvirtuous' Attitudes and Behavior: Reconsidering Negativity, Complaining, Pessimism, and 'False' Hope," *Journal of Clinical Psychology* 9(58): 961–964, https://doi.org/10.1002/jclp.10092.

5. Perry, T. (2004). "The Case of the Toothless Watchdog," *Ethnicities* 4(4): 501–521, https://doi.org/10.1177/1468796804047471.

6. Epictetus. (1995). *Discourses*, 2.5.4. Translated by Robin Hard. London: Everyman.

7. Ibid, 3.22.10.

8. Seppälä, E., Bradley, C., and Goldstein, M. R. (2020). "Research: Why Breathing Is So Effective at Reducing Stress," *Harvard Business Review,* September 29, https://hbr.org/2020/09/research-why-breathing-is-so-effective-at-reducing-stress.

Chapter 5: The Awesome Power of Gratitude

1. Utami, M. S., Shalihah, M., Adhiningtyas, N. P., Rahmah, S., and Ningrum, W. K. (2020). "Gratitude Cognitive Behavior Therapy (G-CBT) to Reduce College Students' Academic Stress," *Jurnal Psikologi* 47(2), August 24, https://jurnal.ugm.ac.id/jpsi/article/view/43730.
2. Durmus, G. (2023). "The Place of Gratitude in an Islamic Bank's Organizational Communication Culture," *Journal of Erciyes Communication* 10(1): 41–56, https://doi.org/10.17680/erciyesiletisim.1189243.
3. Kim, K. (2019). "The Relationship between Perceived Stress and Life Satisfaction of Soldiers: Moderating Effects of Gratitude," *Asia-Pacific Journal of Convergent Research Interchange* 4(5): 1–8, https://doi.org/10.21742/apjcri.2019.12.01.
4. Durmus, "The Place of Gratitude."
5. See Stumpf, T., Califf, C., and Lancaster, J. (2022). "Digital Nomad Entrepreneurship and Lifestyle Design: A Process Theory," Proceedings of the 55th Hawaii International Conference on System Sciences 2002, https://doi.org/10.24251/hicss.2022.634, and Pasdiora, M., Brei, V., and Nicolao, L. (2020). "When Repetitive Consumption Leads to Predictions of Faster Adaptation," *Journal of Consumer Behavior* 5(19): 450–462. https://doi.org/10.1002/cb.1823.
6. Winnick, M. (2016). "Putting a Finger on Our Phone Obsession," People Nerds (dscout blog), June 16, https://dscout.com/people-nerds/mobile-touches.
7. Seligman, M. (2018). *The Hope Circuit: A Psychologist's Journey from Helplessness to Optimism* New York: PublicAffairs, p. 262.
8. Ibid.
9. Utami et al., "Gratitude Cognitive Behavior Therapy."

10. Ibid.
11. Waldinger, R., and Schulz, M. (2023). *The Good Life: Lessons from the World's Longest Scientific Study of Happiness.* New York: Simon and Schuster.
12. Zeng, Z. (2023). "The Theories and Effect of Gratitude: A System Review," *Journal of Education, Humanities, and Social Sciences* 8, 1158–1163.
13. Emmons, R. A., and McCullough, M. E. (2003). "Counting Blessings Versus Burdens: An Experimental Investigation of Gratitude and Subjective Well-Being in Daily Life," *Journal of Personality and Social Psychology* 84(2): 377–389.
14. Bono, G., and Froh, J. (2009). "Gratitude in School: Benefits to Students and Schools," in R. Gilman, E. S. Huebner, and M. J. Furlong (Eds.), *Handbook of Positive Psychology in Schools.* London: Routledge/Taylor & Francis Group, pp. 77–88.

Chapter 6: Reframing Negative Events

1. Tedeschi, R. G., and Calhoun, L. G. (2004). "Posttraumatic Growth: Conceptual Foundations and Empirical Evidence," *Psychological Inquiry* 15(1): 1–18, https://doi.org/10.1207/s15327965pli1501_01.
2. Kishimi, I., and Koga, F. (2018). *The Courage to Be Disliked: The Japanese Phenomenon That Shows You How to Change Your Life and Achieve Real Happiness.* New York: Atria Books.
3. Ibid.
4. Taleb, N. (2012). *Antifragile: Things That Gain from Disorder.* New York: Random House, pp. 31–34.
5. Nietzsche, F. (1997). *Twilight of the Idols.* Indianapolis: Hackett Publishing Company, p. 6.
6. Note that this quote is attributed to Gibran, but it does not appear exactly in his published work.
7. This quote crystallizes a central tenet of Stoicism, but it does not appear exactly in any of Marcus Aurelius's work. It likely is from a translation that paraphrased a key passage in Meditations, Book IV.3.

8. Maurer, M. M., and Daukantaite, D. (2021). "Revisiting the Organismic Valuing Process Theory of Personal Growth: A Theoretical Review of Rogers and Its Connection to Positive Psychology," *Frontiers in Psychology* 12 (June 3): 1706. https://pubmed.ncbi.nlm.nih.gov/32793057/.

9. Ibid.

10. Joseph, S., and Linley, P. A. (2005). "Positive Adjustment to Threatening Events: An Organismic Valuing Theory of Growth through Adversity," *Review of General Psychology* 9(3): 262–280, https://doi.org/10.1037/1089-2680.9.3.262.

11. Ibid.

12. Dell'Osso, L., et al. (2023). "Biological Correlates of Post-Traumatic Growth (PTG): A Literature Review," *Brain Sciences* 13(2): 305, https://doi.org/10.3390/brainsci13020305.

13. Walsh, D., et al. (2018). "A Model to Predict Psychological- and Health-Related Adjustment in Men with Prostate Cancer: The Role of Post Traumatic Growth, Physical Post Traumatic Growth, Resilience and Mindfulness," *Frontiers in Psychology* 9, https://www.ncbi.nlm.nih.gov/pmc/articles/PMC5818687/.

Chapter 7: How to Live Happily with Political Divisiveness

1. Hoffer, E. (1951). *Thoughts on the Nature of Mass Movements.* New York: Harper & Brothers.

2. Ibid.

3. Ibid.

4. Gray, D. (2016). *Liminal Thinking: Create the Change You Want by Changing the Way You Think.* New York: Two Waves Books.

5. Rozado, D., Hughes, R., and Halberstadt, J. (2022). "Longitudinal Analysis of Sentiment and Emotion in News Media Headlines Using Automated Labelling with Transformer Language Models," *PLoS ONE* 17(10, October 18), https://doi.org/10.1371/journal.pone.0276367.

6. Ibid.

7. Smith, K. B. (2022). "Politics Is Making Us Sick: The Negative Impact of Political Engagement on Public Health During the Trump Administration," *PLoS ONE* 17(1), https://doi.org/10.1371/journal .pone.0262022.
8. Ibid.
9. Ibid.
10. Abramowitz, A., and Webster, S. (2018). "Negative Partisanship: Why Americans Dislike Parties But Behave Like Rabid Partisans," *Advances in Political Psychology* 39(Supp. 1), https://doi.org/10.1111/ pops.12479.
11. Ibid.
12. Ibid.

Chapter 8: Wanting and the Perils of Social Media

1. Burgis, L. (2021). *Wanting: The Power of Mimetic Desire in Everyday Life.* New York: St. Martin's Press.
2. Ibid.
3. Ibid.
4. Digital Citizen Academy. (n.d.). "Finsta: Does Your Child Have a Secret Instagram Account?" https://digitalcitizenacademy.org/ finsta-does-your-child-have-a-secret-instagram-account/.
5. Best Day Psychiatry and Consulting. (n.d.). "The Effects of Bullying on Mental Health," https://bestdaypsych.com/the-effects-of- bullying-on-mental-health/.
6. Wang, J., Nansel, T., and Iannotti, R. (2011). "Cyber and Traditional Bullying: Differential Association with Depression," *Journal of Adolescent Health* 48(4): 415–417, https://doi.org/10.1016/j .jadohealth.2010.07.012.
7. Lickteig, B. (n.d.). "Social Media: Cyberbullying, Body Shaming, and Trauma," Child Advocacy Center of Lapeer County, https://caclapeer.org/social-media-cyberbullying-body-shaming- and-trauma/.
8. Kowalski, R., and Limber, S. (2013). "Psychological, Physical, and Academic Correlates of Cyberbullying and Traditional Bullying,"

Journal of Adolescent Health 53(1) Supplement, S13–S20, https://doi.org/10.1016/j.jadohealth.2012.09.018.

9. Robertson, R., et al. (2023). "Users choose to engage with more partisan news than they are exposed to on Google Search," *Nature* 618, 342–348, https://www.nature.com/articles/s41586-023-06078-5; Barrett, P., Hendrix, J., and Sims, G. (2021). "How Social Media Fuels U.S. Political Polarization—What to Do about It," The Hill, https://thehill.com/opinion/campaign/572002-how-social-media-fuels-us-political-polarization-what-to-do-about-it/; Huszar, F., et al. (2021). "Algorithmic Amplification of Politics on Twitter," *Proceedings of the National Academy of Sciences* 119(1), https://doi.org/10.1073/pnas.2025334119.

10. Robertson, R., et al. (2023). "Users choose to engage with more partisan news than they are exposed to on Google Search," *Nature* 618, 342–348, https://www.nature.com/articles/s41586-023-06078-5.

11. Kleinman, Z. (2021). "Political Trolling Twice as Popular as Positivity, Study Suggests," BBC.com, June 21, https://www.bbc.com/news/technology-57558028.

12. Laub, Z. (2019). "Hate Speech on Social Media: Global Comparisons," Council on Foreign Relations, June 7, https://www.cfr.org/backgrounder/hate-speech-social-media-global-comparisons.

13. Cinelli, M., et al. (2021). "The Echo Chamber Effect on Social Media," *Proceedings of the National Academy of Sciences* 118(9), https://doi.org/10.1073/pnas.2023301118.

14. Matthews, D. (2023). "Why the news is so negative—and what we can do about it," Vox, March 22, https://www.vox.com/the-highlight/23596969/bad-news-negativity-bias-media.

15. Peterson, J. (2018). "Rule 2: "Treat Yourself Like Someone You Are Responsible for Helping," *12 Rules for Life: An Antidote to Chaos*. Random House Canada, pp. 31–66.

16. Dunbar, R. (1997). *Grooming, Gossip, and the Evolution of Language*. Cambridge, MA: Harvard University Press, p. 137.

17. Georgiev, D., and Defensor, G. (2023). "How Much Time Do People Spend on Social Media in 2023?" Techjury, June 23, https://techjury.net/blog/time-spent-on-social-media/.

18. Harari, Y. (2017). "The Meaning of Life in a World Without Work," *Guardian*, May 8, https://www.theguardian.com/technology/2017/may/08/virtual-reality-religion-robots-sapiens-book.

19. Kelly, S. (2022). "TikTok May Push Potentially Harmful Content to Teens Within Minutes, Study Finds," CNN Business, December 15, https://www.cnn.com/2022/12/15/tech/tiktok-teens-study-trnd/index.html.

20. Beyens, I., et al. (2020). "Social Media Use and Adolescents' Well-Being: Developing a Typology of Person-Specific Effect Patterns," *PsyArXiv*, December 16, https://doi.org/10.31234/osf.io/ftygp.

21. Cook, S., et al. (2021). "Increases in Serious Psychological Distress Among Ontario Students Between 2013 and 2017: Assessing the Impact of Time Spent on Social Media," *Canadian Journal of Psychiatry* 8(66), 747–756, https://doi.org/10.1177/0706743720987902.ftygp.

22. Bellovary, A., Young, N., and Goldenberg, A. (2021). "Left- and Right-Leaning News Organizations' Negative Tweets Are More Likely to Be Shared," *PsyArXiv*, February 24, https://doi.org/10.31234/osf.io/2er67.

23. Kross, E., et al. (2021). "Social Media and Well-Being: Pitfalls, Progress, and Next Steps," *Trends in Cognitive Sciences* 1(25, November 10): 55–66, https://doi.org/10.1016/j.tics.2020.10.005.

Chapter 9: How to Change Your State

1. Department of Health, State Government of Victoria, Australia (n.d.). "Breathing the Reduce Stress," Better Health Channel, https://www.betterhealth.vic.gov.au/health/healthyliving/breathing-to-reduce-stress#.

2. Gross, J. J., and Levenson, R. W. (1993). "Emotional Suppression: Physiology, Self-report, and Expressive Behavior," *Journal of Personality and Social Psychology* 6(64): 970–986, https://doi.org/10.1037/0022-3514.64.6.970.

3. Thoma, M. V., et al. (2014). "Effects of Music Listening on Pre-Treatment Anxiety and Stress Levels in a Dental Hygiene Recall Population," *International Journal of Behavioral Medicine* 22(4): 498–505, doi:10.1007/s12529-014-9439-x.

4. Terry, P. C., Karageorghis, C. I., Curran, M. L., Martin, O. V., and Parsons-Smith, R. L. (2020). "Effects of Music in Exercise and Sport: A Meta-analytic Review," *Psychological Bulletin* 146(2): 91–117, https://doi.org/10.1037/bul0000216.

5. Wang, C., Bannuru, R. R., Ramel, J., Kupelnick, B., Scott, T., and Schmid, C. H. (2010). "Tai Chi on Psychological Well-being: Systematic Review and Meta-analysis," *BMC Complement Altern Med* 1(10), https://doi.org/10.1186/1472-6882-10-23.

6. Zou, L., Sasaki, J. E., Wei, G., et al. (2018). "Effects of Mind–Body Exercises (Tai Chi/Yoga) on Heart Rate Variability Parameters and Perceived Stress: A Systematic Review with Meta-analysis of Randomized Controlled Trials," *JCM* 11(7): 404, https://doi.org/10.3390/jcm7110404.

7. Terry et al., "Effects of Music."

8. Yim, J. (2016). "Therapeutic Benefits of Laughter in Mental Health: A Theoretical Review," *Tohoku Journal of Experimental Medicine* 239(3): 243–249, https://pubmed.ncbi.nlm.nih.gov/27439375/.

9. Dunbar, R. (2016). *Human Evolution: Our Brains and Behavior.* Oxford University Press.

10. Rancour P. (2017) "The Emotional Freedom Technique: Finally, a Unifying Theory for the Practice of Holistic Nursing, or Too Good to Be True?" *Journal of Holistic Nursing* 35(4): 382–388. doi: 10.1177/0898010116648456.

11. Liu, L. (2016). "A Poetic Duet: While Sleep Is the Best Meditation, Writing Is the Best Medication," Medium, October 22, https://lauraliuk3.medium.com/writing-is-the-best-medication-59ab40e5934a.

12. Seligman, M. (2006). *Learned Optimism: How to Change Your Mind and Your Life.* New York: Penguin Random House.

13. Ibid.

Chapter 10: Minding Mindfulness

1. Steig, C. (2020). "Oprah, Ray Dalio and Lady Gaga swear by this simple meditation technique," CNBC.com, January 7, https://www.cnbc.com/2020/01/06/celebs-who-do-transcendental-meditation-oprah-ray-dalio-lady-gaga.html.

2. Hill, C. G., and Updegraff, J. A. (2012). "Mindfulness and Its Relationship to Emotional Regulation," *Emotion* 1(12): 81–90, https://doi.org/10.1037/a0026355.

3. Mrazek, M. D., Franklin, M. S., Phillips, D.T., Baird, B., and Schooler, J. W. (2013). "Mindfulness Training Improves Working Memory Capacity and GRE Performance While Reducing Mind Wandering," *Psychological Science* 5(24): 776–781, https://doi.org/10.1177/0956797612459659.

4. Albrecht, N. J. (2018). "Teachers Teaching Mindfulness with Children: Being a Mindful Role Model," *Australian Journal of Teacher Education* 43(10), https://ro.ecu.edu.au/ajte/vol43/iss10/1.

5. Linder, J. (2019). "How Mindfulness Can Reshape Negative Thought Patterns," *Psychology Today*, April 18, https://www.psychologytoday.com/us/blog/mindfulness-insights/201904/how-mindfulness-can-reshape-negative-thought-patterns.

6. Prax, A. (2020). "How to Release Anxiety Using Breath," Yogapedia.com, March 30, https://www.yogapedia.com/2/9598/breath/breathing-techniques/how-to-release-anxiety-using-breath.

7. Mindfulness.com. (n.d.). "4 Steps to Overcome Negative Thoughts," https://mindfulness.com/mindful-living/overcome-negative-thoughts.

8. Mindfulness.com. (n.d.). "Name It to Tame It: Label Your Emotions to Overcome Negative Thoughts," https://mindfulness.com/mindful-living/name-it-to-tame-it.

9. Ivtzan, I., et al. (2016). "Integrating Mindfulness into Positive Psychology: A Randomised Controlled Trial of an Online Positive Mindfulness Program," *Mindfulness* 7, 1396–1407, https://link.springer.com/article/10.1007/s12671-016-0581-1.

10. Zeidan, F., et al. (2015). "Mindfulness Meditation-based Pain Relief Employs Different Neural Mechanisms Than Placebo and Sham Mindfulness Meditation-induced Analgesia," *Journal of Neuroscience* 46(35): 15307–15325, https://doi.org/10.1523/jneurosci.2542-15.2015.

11. Kiken, L. G., et al. (2015). "From a State to a Trait: Trajectories of State Mindfulness in Meditation During Intervention Predict Changes in Trait Mindfulness," *Personality and Individual Differences* 81(July): 41–46, https://doi.org/10.1016/j.paid.2014.12.044.

12. Fortney, L., et al. (2013). "Abbreviated Mindfulness Intervention for Job Satisfaction, Quality of Life, and Compassion in Primary Care Clinicians: A Pilot Study," *Annals of Family Medicine* 5(11): 412–420, https://doi.org/10.1370/afm.1511.
13. Schlosser, M., Jones, R., Demnitz-King, H., and Marchant, N. L. (2020). "Meditation Experience Is Associated with Lower Levels of Repetitive Negative Thinking: The Key Role of Self-Compassion." *Curr Psychol* 5(41): 3144–3155. https://doi.org/10.1007/s12144-020-00839-5.

Chapter 11: How to Forget Your Problems and Concerns

1. Wise, R., and Robble, M. (2020), "Dopamine and Addiction," *Annual Review of Psychology* 4(71): 79–106, https://pubmed.ncbi.nlm.nih.gov/31905114/.
2. Solon, O. (2017). "Ex-Facebook President Sean Parker: Site Made to Exploit Human Vulnerability," *Guardian*, November 9, https://www.theguardian.com/technology/2017/nov/09/facebook-sean-parker-vulnerability-brain-psychology.
3. Weinstein, N., and Ryan, R. (2010). "When Helping Helps: Autonomous Motivation for Prosocial Behavior and Its Influence on Well-being for the Helper and Recipient," *Journal of Personality and Social Psychology* 2(98): 222–244, https://doi.org/10.1037/a0016984.
4. Lanaj, K., and Jennings, R. E. (2020). "Putting Leaders in a Bad Mood: The Affective Costs of Helping Followers with Personal Problems," *Journal of Applied Psychology* 4(105): 355–371, https://doi.org/10.1037/apl0000450.
5. Ibid.

Chapter 12: The Negativity Fast

1. Caprariello, P. A., and Reis, H. T. (2013). "To Do, to Have, or to Share? Valuing Experiences Over Material Possessions Depends on the Involvement of Others," *Journal of Personality and Social Psychology* 2(104): 199–215, https://doi.org/10.1037/a0030953.

2. Fischer, M. A., et al. (2010). "Primary Medication Non-adherence: Analysis of 195,930 Electronic Prescriptions," *Journal of General Internal Medicine* 4(25): 284–290. https://doi.org/10.1007/s11606-010-1253-9.

3. Brown, M. T., and Bussell, J. K. (2011). "Medication Adherence: Who Cares?" *Mayo Clinic Proceedings* 4(86): 304–314, https://doi.org/10.4065/mcp.2010.0575.

4. Spencer, C. (2021), "Some Americans Take Better Care of Their Pets Than Themselves: Poll," The Hill, July 1, https://thehill.com/changing-america/well-being/longevity/561119-some-americans-take-better-care-of-their-pets-than/.

5. Cipolla, C. M. (2021). *The Basic Laws of Human Stupidity.* New York: Doubleday.

6. Parker, P. (2020). *The Art of Gathering: How We Meet and Why It Matters.* New York: Penguin.

Recommended Resources

THERE ARE NUMEROUS mental health communities across social media platforms like Reddit, Instagram, and Facebook. However, while these can be supportive spaces, they should not be used as a substitute for professional help.

Remember that different resources will be helpful for different people, and what works best will depend on a person's individual situation and needs. It's also worth noting that while these resources can be very helpful, they're not a substitute for professional help. If someone is struggling with their mental health, it's important that they reach out to a health-care provider.

Websites

- National Institute of Mental Health (NIMH): The NIMH provides comprehensive information about different mental health conditions and resources.

- MentalHealth.gov: This US government website provides information about mental health, how to get help, and resources for loved ones.
- Anxiety and Depression Association of America (ADAA): The ADAA provides information about these conditions, as well as resources for finding therapists and support groups.
- Substance Abuse and Mental Health Services Administration (SAMHSA): SAMHSA provides a wide range of information about substance abuse and mental health issues.

Online Therapy

- BetterHelp: This online platform provides direct-to-consumer access to behavioral health services.
- TalkSpace: TalkSpace offers online therapy with licensed therapists.
- 7 Cups: This online service connects people to trained volunteers for emotional support and counseling.
- Headspace: This app provides mindfulness and meditation resources, which can be helpful for managing stress, anxiety, and depression.

Books

- *Feeling Good: The New Mood Therapy* by David D. Burns
- *The Upward Spiral* by Alex Korb
- *Wherever You Go, There You Are* by Jon Kabat-Zinn
- *The Body Keeps the Score* by Bessel van der Kolk

Self-Help Resources

- MoodGym: An interactive self-help book that helps you to learn and practice skills that can help to prevent and manage symptoms of depression and anxiety
- Calm: A mindfulness app that offers meditations, sleep stories, breathing programs, stretching exercises, and relaxing music
- MindShift: A mental health app designed to help users cope with anxiety

About the Author

Anthony Iannarino is an American author, sales and leadership expert, and international keynote speaker. He is the author of four books on the modern sales approach, one book on sales leadership, and *The Negativity Fast*. Anthony writes daily at www.thesalesblog.com, where he has published more than 5,000 articles on sales, business, leadership, social issues, and human culture. Born and educated in Columbus, Ohio, Anthony graduated from Capital University, Capital Law School, and Harvard Business School's Owner/President Management Program.

Index

Meditations (Marcus Aurelius), 66
Meditation, value, 158
Memes
  'impact, 119, 124–125
  infection, 124
  spreading, 120
Memetic desire, escape, 134–135
Memetic infections, 118–119
Mental energy, focus, 193–194
Mental health
  impact, 134
  improvement, 87, 91
  issues, increase, 13
Mental state, change, 152
Mental tapes, 171–172
Mimetics, 133–134
Mindful appreciation, practice, 95
Mindfulness
  benefits, evidence, 173
  daily life, 170–171
  importance, 171–173
  meditation, practice, 169
  practicing, 168, 173–175
  science, 175
Misinformation
  impact, 10
  perpetuation, 137–138
Misophonia, self-diagnosis
  (trigger), 198–199
Monday, complaining
  (cessation), 64–65
Money
  giving, 181
  issues, 195–196
Morrison, Jim, 52
Murdoch, Rupert, 116
Musashi, Miyamoto, 175
Music, impact, 154
Musk, Elon, 14, 69
My problem (MP), 67–68

N
Name It to Tame It, 172
Narrative
  creation, 103

domination, 121
  need, 123
Natural occurrences, 195
Nature therapy, 155
Negative differentiation, 4
Negative dominance, 4
Negative events
  impact, 86
  reframing, 162, 204
Negative experiences, 32, 94, 161
  impact, 103, 106
  meaning, search, 110
  reframing, 66
  right, claim, 17
Negative feeling, 157
Negative gradients, steepness, 4
Negative loop, 63–64
Negative opinions, 28
Negative people, trigger, 199–200
Negative postings, avoidance, 146
Negative potency, 4
Negative social media, avoidance,
  143–144
Negative state
  creation, 21
  escape, talking (usage), 30
  journaling, 202–203
  removal, 153
Negative state, prevention, 153
Negative surprises, 191
Negative thinking, repetition, 175
Negative thoughts
  attention, 161
  challenge, 161–162
Negativity
  absence, 51
  avoidance, 191
  bias, 79, 163–164
    overcoming, 84
    reduction, 187
    usage, 138
  biological component/sources, 10–12
  cause, fears (impact), 50
  conversation, example, 23
  escape, 88, 152